Sociology Transformed

Series Editors
John Holmwood
School of Sociology and Social Policy
University of Nottingham
Nottingham, UK

Stephen Turner
Department of Philosophy
University of South Florida
Tampa, FL, USA

The field of sociology has changed rapidly over the last few decades. Sociology Transformed seeks to map these changes on a country by country basis and to contribute to the discussion of the future of the subject. The series is concerned not only with the traditional centres of the discipline, but with its many variant forms across the globe.

Sayana Mitupova • Koji Yoshino

Sociology in Japan

The Overlooked Trajectory of Its Development

Sayana Mitupova
The Russian Academy of National
Economy and Public
Administration — RANEPA
Moscow, Russia

Koji Yoshino
Nagasaki Wesleyan University
Isahaya, Nagasaki, Japan

ISSN 2947-5023   ISSN 2947-5031   (electronic)
Sociology Transformed
ISBN 978-3-031-91346-4   ISBN 978-3-031-91347-1   (eBook)
https://doi.org/10.1007/978-3-031-91347-1

This Palgrave Macmillan imprint is published by the registered company Springer Nature Switzerland AG.
The registered company address is: Gewerbestrasse 11, 6330 Cham, Switzerland

If disposing of this product, please recycle the paper.

PREFACE

The authors have long studied the history of Japanese sociology. However, we were compelled to compile this work intensively under time constraints. Furthermore, we were troubled by space limitations. Depending on where one places the origins of sociology, even if we limit ourselves to the history of Japanese sociology influenced by sociology since A. Comte, it spans nearly 150 years. Beyond the sociologists featured in this book, Japan has produced many other excellent sociologists. Moreover, most of them are unknown even by name in the global sociological community. If we were to include all their names, we would either run out of space entirely or end up with a mere index-like listing of names. Therefore, we decided on one principle: this book would spotlight representative figures of each era and depict the history of Japanese sociology through their research. This was our last resort for writing a compact yet substantive history of sociology.

Another limitation is that we have devoted considerable space to pre-war sociology. As mentioned earlier, this is partly because pre-war Japanese sociology was largely unknown internationally, with only a few scholars active on the global stage. More importantly, however, post-war Japanese sociology is a major theme that deserves independent treatment, and there exists a discontinuity that prevents us from discussing it in the same context as in the pre-war period. As is well known, Japan, defeated in the Pacific War, was under Allied occupation for seven years. During this period, the purge of educators and writing system reforms were implemented. These two factors created a significant generational gap between pre-war and post-war scholars. The generation that received higher education after the war felt betrayed by the pre-war generation. Many criticized pre-war sociology, and some formed Marxist schools of sociology. The course of post-war Japanese sociology is also a history of these conflicts. While such ideological conflicts no longer exist today, there is also no unified perspective; although the field is thriving, researchers are approaching their subjects with their own methods and focuses. It is simply impossible to fully discuss these developments in a small volume like this book.

Of course, this book does include one or two chapters dealing with the post-war period. Many of the sociologists discussed there received their sociological education before the war and had varying degrees of connection to the pre-war era. While we aspire to write *Sociology in Japan After 1945* focusing on post-independence Japanese sociology, it would likely be quite different in both style and tone from this book.

Despite these limitations, we are greatly honored that this book will reach the eyes of sociologists worldwide. While global sociology needs unified theories on a global scale, it equally requires diverse, vernacular developments. The history of Japanese sociology, which has incorporated various countries' sociological traditions while experiencing its own developments and setbacks, may serve as a case study for understanding the future direction of global sociology.

We earnestly hope that global sociologists who embody the theoretical accumulation of Japanese sociology introduced in this book will pursue ever deeper analyses of Japanese society. This will surely result in valuable work that transcends superficial, journalistic theories about Japanese society. Nothing would make us happier than if this book could contribute to that end.

Moscow, Russia   Sayana Mitupova
Isahaya, Nagasaki, Japan   Koji Yoshino

ACKNOWLEDGMENTS

We wish to extend our appreciation to the series editors John Holmwood and Stephen Turner, and the anonymous reviewers at the initial stage of this project. Their constructive feedback and thoughtful critiques were helpful in refining our ideas and enhancing the overall quality of the manuscript. We would also like to express our gratitude to Professor Shujiro Yazawa for his invaluable long-term guidance and support throughout our academic journeys. His insights and expertise in sociology have greatly enriched our understanding and shaped the direction of our work.

Additionally, the authors wish to express their profound gratitude to their teachers, without whom their career paths would not have been possible: Professor Yoshinobu Yanagita (Japan) and Professor Vladimir Kultygin (Russia).

Finally, we would like to acknowledge our families and friends for their support and patience during the writing process. Their encouragement has been vital to the completion of this work.

CONTENTS

CHAPTER 1

Introduction

Abstract For Japan, all modern sciences were imported disciplines. Sociology, too, was brought about through the influx of European culture. The history of Japanese sociology generally begins with the introduction of Auguste Comte's (1798–1857) ideas by students sent to study in the Netherlands during the late Edo period, followed by the introduction of Herbert Spencer's (1820–1903) theories in the early Meiji period. As discussed below, these undoubtedly had an enormous influence on Japanese sociology. However, it would be incorrect to say that there were no disciplines similar to sociology within Japanese thought before this time. Japan's ability to accept and establish sociology was due to nothing other than this country's social conditions and, more specifically, the foundation of its academic and intellectual traditions. To discuss only the aspect of sociology as an imported discipline while ignoring these factors would be entirely insufficient as an explanation of Japanese sociology's history. Therefore, this chapter will address not only the influx of foreign culture but also Japan's history of science and intellectual history that formed its foundation.

Keywords Indigenous culture (Dochaku Bunka) • Western learning (Rangaku) • Confucianism • Transplantation of knowledge • Auguste Comte • John Stuart Mill • National seclusion • Meiji enlightenment

S. Mitupova, K. Yoshino, *Sociology in Japan*, Sociology Transformed, https://doi.org/10.1007/978-3-031-91347-1_1

1

Indigenous and Foreign Cultures

Generally, the influx of culture is determined by the conditions of the receiving society. When there is sufficient readiness, subsequent acceptance occurs swiftly. Here, readiness refers to whether a society has adequately developed its capacity for social awareness, value consciousness, receptivity to foreign cultures, and critical thinking about them. For Japan, Western sociology was not necessarily an entirely alien or unknown entity beyond imagination. The influx of Western sociology into Japan could be said to have been adapted, in a sense, onto Japan's traditional intellectual foundation.

This raises the following questions: Did sociological scientific thought exist within Japanese intellectual history? If it did exist, how can it be evaluated? Furthermore, how did it merge with Western sociology? This chapter will address these issues.

What we mean by sociological scientific thought generally encompasses the following thought patterns. First is social realism, that is, the attitude of recognizing and evaluating social reality. Sociology cannot exist without acknowledging the existence of society beyond oneself. Second is objectivism. Sociology cannot be established without maintaining a certain distance from society. Third is sociological collectivism. Sociology cannot exist without recognizing society as an entity that is more than just a collection of individuals, one that constitutes its own phenomenal world (Durkheim's social facts). Fourth, systems thinking is essential for sociology. Social phenomena must be understood not as existing individually but as forming a coherent system. In terms of such sociological thinking, Japan had Confucian thought imported from China even before Western science was introduced. At the beginning of the Edo period, Confucian studies constituted almost all academic pursuits. By the mid-Edo period in the eighteenth century, scientific thinking centered on medicine and military science flowed in from the Netherlands. These Chinese and Dutch studies occupy important positions in the establishment of Japanese sociology.

Stimulation of Japan's Intellectual Tradition

How did Western civilization influence Japanese ways of thinking about society? This period can be divided into three stages. In the first stage, knowledge of Western social reality itself fostered Japanese people's objective and critical attitudes toward social reality. In the second stage, causal recognition of social reality was introduced—the emergence of analytical thinking about society. After this preparatory stage, the third stage finally arrived with the adoption of systematic Western social science and sociology.

The Japanese people, who had maintained isolation for a long time during the Edo period, were cut off from contact with external societies and had little knowledge of different social systems. Such circumstances tend to make people view their own social system as self-evident and immutable. Conversely, it is very difficult to gain an attitude of maintaining distance from society and observing it objectively. The Japanese people of the Edo period overcame these limitations of isolated thinking through two factors: the study of history and critical spirit toward social contradictions and irrationalities. Looking back at history, various political systems appeared and disappeared. This knowledge cultivated an eye for viewing society relatively and objectively. Even during the isolation period, knowledge of Western society could be obtained through Dutch residents. Although this knowledge was limited, it provided a comparative perspective with Western social reality and a viewpoint for criticizing Japanese society.[1]

The main positions critics relied on were mercantilism and nationalism. Mercantilists criticized the agrarian self-sufficient economy. Toshiaki Honda (1743–1821) is famous as a representative of Japanese mercantilism. In his *Tale of Western Regions* (1798), he introduced to Japan the reality of how Western nations achieved stability through maritime trade.[2] Furthermore, he independently published arguments similar to Malthus's *An Essay on the Principle of Population* (1798) during the same period. According to him, the population would increase 19.75 times in 33 years, but land productivity would fall short of this. Therefore, he concluded that an inevitable imbalance would arise between population and means of subsistence.

Moreover, Seika Fujiwara (1561–1619) argued in his *Shipboard Regulations* (1603) that overseas trade benefits not only one's own country but also trading partners. He went further to state that in overseas trade, legal order forms even between countries that cannot communicate through language. This view was remarkably close to that of Grotius (1583–1645).

Next came criticism from the nationalist camp regarding deficiencies in external military systems. Isolation led Japanese people to believe that

Japan was the entire world. In other words, it made them forget that Japan existed within the world. Shihei Hayashi (1738–1793) attempted to correct this mistaken view. He traveled throughout the country studying geography and had opportunities to contact Dutch people in Nagasaki. Through this, he faced the reality that Japan was in imminent danger of invasion. He explained the vulnerability of Japan's outdated military equipment relying on horses, bows, and swords, and argued for the urgency of national defense in international relations. The intensity of his arguments led the Edo shogunate to consider him a person of concern, but the reality of tense world circumstances added persuasiveness to his claims. While he certainly cautioned against overemphasis on military force, his statements were not merely advocating for peace. They came from the urgent feeling that national defense could not be entrusted to old-fashioned, crude warriors. The introduction of advanced foreign defense systems was urgent.

Such tense circumstances surrounding Japan instilled nationalism[3] in the Japanese people. Mokichi Fujita's (1852–1892) *History of Civilization's Eastward Advance* (1884) analyzed this fact early on, stating that when Britain invaded China in the Opium War of 1840, neighboring Japan remembered the concept of 'our nation' which it had temporarily forgotten (Mokichi Fujita, *History of Civilization's Eastward Advance*, Chapter 17 'New Strategies for National Protection').

As shown above, contact with Western civilization taught Japanese people an objective attitude toward observing society. However, we must not forget what existed at the foundation of this objective recognition and critical ability—namely, the rationalistic spirit that Japanese people had cultivated since ancient times. This determined the direction of Japanese scientific history in choosing medicine and military science when absorbing Dutch learning. These undoubtedly form part of the background for the establishment of sociology.

THE YAMANOTE SCHOOL OF DUTCH STUDIES

Following the highly practical Western arts such as medicine and military science, Western science was introduced to Japan. Sociology's founder A. Comte distinguished science into mathematics, astronomy, physics, chemistry, biology, and sociology, predicting that sociology would come after the development of natural sciences, both theoretically and historically. Coincidentally, this process of scientific development also applies to the personal experiences of modern science pioneers in Japan. For example, Yoan Udagawa (1798–1846) and Genpo Mitsukuri (1799–1863), who started as researchers of Western natural science, gradually shifted their interests to humanities such as Western history in their later years. Furthermore, among the group of natural scientists studying Dutch learning centered on medicine, some scholars gradually shifted their interests to political and social issues. For example, in the group of Dutch scholars known as the Yamanote School, which included Sanei Koseki (1787–1839), Choei Takano (1804–1850), Kazan Watanabe (1793–1841), and Nobuhiro Sato (1769–1850) (Mokichi Fujita, *History of Civilization's Eastward Advance*, Chapter 7 'The Power of Practical Learning in Various Arts').

Systematic knowledge about society and state was first received in the field of geography. Choei Takano stated that Western geography revealed world governance, warfare, the rise and fall of nations, customs, and traditions. Kazan Watanabe argued that while Western learning was thought to study physical laws, it could actually be applied not only to material phenomena but also to social phenomena (*Seiyo Jijyo Tosyo*). According to Watanabe, the three fields of geography discussed by Sanei Koseki included theoretical and measurement research, natural historical research, and state studies.

Through the activities of the Yamanote School of Dutch Studies, Japanese social awareness deepened rapidly. This was based on understanding geographical situations from military interests. Going further back, it could also be attributed to Japanese people's strong curiosity about geography and climate. Since the Muromachi period, books titled *Jinkokuki*[4] had been written continuously in Japan, recording the social conditions and customs of people across Japan. The addition of Western geography to this tradition likely strengthened Japanese people's analytical capability regarding society.

The aforementioned three scholars—Koseki, Takano, and Watanabe—ultimately faced suppression by the shogunate and were executed, which was unfortunate for the development of sociology's history. Their names must be remembered as pioneers of Japanese sociology.

Fukuzawa's Sociological Thought

In the late Edo period (after 1850), Western information flowed in steadily. The representative intellectual of this era was Yukichi Fukuzawa (1835–1901). He was a thinker and educator who introduced Western social conditions, devoted himself to importing learning, and developed theories about Japanese society. In his main work, *An Outline of a Theory of Civilization* (1875), Fukuzawa explained that social changes follow laws that can be captured through statistical methods. Based on Henry Thomas Buckle (1821–1862) of England and François Pierre Guillaume Guizot (1787–1874) of France, he discussed the flow of Western civilization and positioned Japan within it. He argued that Japan had a state but no nation and advocated for the establishment of individuality, believing that individual power brings about civilization's progress.

This thinking was further advanced in his *On Decentralization* (1877). There, he posited that the power of human minds brought about by the Meiji Restoration was the determining factor in social movements. Fukuzawa focused particularly on the former samurai class. He explained that the momentum of samurai power continued to dominate Japan even after the Meiji Restoration, albeit in different forms. This was because, like the law of inertia, momentum continues for a certain period. However, this power underwent changes. Specifically, it is divided into three parts. First were the promoters of restoration reforms and civilization enlightenment—the darlings of the era who would eventually turn to conservatism. Second were those who promoted reforms like the first group but had not secured firm social positions, typically represented by civil rights activists seeking public political participation. The third power holders were conservatives (traditionalists). Fukuzawa's sociological insight can be seen in how he analyzed society by breaking down the former samurai group into these three forces rather than treating them as a single group.

Furthermore, in *On the Current Situation* (1882), published five years after the above work, Fukuzawa keenly perceived how the civil rights movement of the second group had succeeded and how their claims had evolved from human rights to suffrage rights. He identified the main causes of this rising trend as: (1) the establishment of local assemblies, (2) the abolition of domains and establishment of prefectures along with land tax reforms, and (3) education. Such analysis thoroughly demonstrates Fukuzawa's analytical capabilities as a sociologist.

The Introduction of A. Comte and J.S. Mill to Japan: Key Figures

If Yukichi Fukuzawa analyzed Japanese society using Western sociological methods, it was Amane Nishi (1829–1897) who systematically introduced academic knowledge of philosophy, law, economics, and sociology to Japan. Along with Mamichi Tsuda (1829–1903), he stayed in the Netherlands as a student sent by the Edo shogunate in 1863. They studied natural law, international law, national law, economics, and statistics under Simon Vissering (1818–1888) at Leiden University. Tsuda published these lectures as a translation titled *Theory of Western State Law* (1868). Meanwhile, Nishi introduced Vissering's theories in his book *International Law* (1868).

These two were Japan's earliest introducers of Comte. This introduction was mediated by Dutch philosopher Cornelis Willem Opzoomer (1821–1892), then at Utrecht University. Teaching there since 1846, he was devoted to Comte and John Stuart Mill (1806–1873). Through Opzoomer's teachings, Tsuda and Nishi became indirectly familiar with Comte and Mill.

Here, let us briefly review the relationship between Comte and Mill in Western sociology's history. Comte and Mill maintained a friendship through correspondence, mutually stimulating each other's academic thoughts. One attraction of Comte's *Course in Positive Philosophy* was its positioning of sociology within the overall system of sciences. Mill further developed this thinking, discussing methodology from natural science to sociology. Mill clarified the distinction between social dynamics and statics in sociology (J.S. Mill 1843 *A System of Logic*). He agreed with Comte's so-called three-stage theory, emphasizing, like Comte, the progression of human nature and the importance of knowledge and education (J.S. Mill 1861, *Utilitarianism*). However, Mill was skeptical of Comte's ultimately proposed Religion of Humanity. Mill believed that the Religion of Humanity might possess psychological power and social effectiveness equivalent to religion without the existence of God. From Mill's thoroughly secular perspective, Comte's Religion of Humanity was a dangerous ideology that could deprive individuals of freedom and individuality. How did Nishi convey this sociology of Comte and Mill to Japan?

Nishi frequently referred to Western scientific classification theories, particularly noting Comte's academic classification theory. This was not merely a classification method but an orderly academic system progressing from abstract basic theory to applied theory observing concrete objects.[5]

After the Meiji Restoration, various sciences flowed abundantly into Japan from abroad. Nishi took on the role of eagerly absorbing and introducing these to Japan. In doing so, he keenly felt the need to organize these diverse sciences, making a classification system essential. This explains Nishi's special interest in scientific classification. However, he did not introduce Comte's sociology in detail. Rather, Nishi discussed Mill's work with genuine sympathy, evidenced by his translation of *Utilitarianism* (Mill 1861). This translation by Nishi, titled *Rigaku* (1877), was rendered entirely in classical Chinese. This too reflects the academic situation in Japan at that time. To establish Western sociology within Japanese academia, the use of traditional Confucian terminology was convenient.[6] The Confucian scholar who assisted with this Chinese translation was Rouro Sakatani (1822–1881).

While Nishi was Comte's first introducer, his treatment was quite limited. In contrast, Tongo Takebe (1871–1945), a professor at Tokyo Imperial University, placed complete trust in Comte's sociology and worked to establish it in Japan. Having studied in France, he was devoted to Comte's sociology. Meanwhile, Takebe also considered Confucianism essentially sociological. Therefore, his four-volume masterwork *General Sociology* (1904) attempted to integrate Comte's thought with Confucian ideology. Takebe's sociology was characterized by its emphasis on familial and hierarchical order, based on positivist spirit and organic social views. This can be glimpsed in his use of Confucian scholar Lu Xiangshan's concepts of 'principle' and 'force' to explain social dynamics (*Ten Lectures on Applied Sociology* 1927).

Meiji Japan's sociological thought connected Confucianism with Western sociology. This was natural because Western thought researchers at the time were versed in Confucianism. However, it was also because Confucian thought itself contained elements compatible with Western sociology. In Confucianism, realism and rationalism create norms for human relationships. It taught morality separated from religion, such as loyalty to lords, filial piety to parents, social justice, and love for companions. Such Confucian thought could easily integrate with Western modern rationalism. Western intellectual history was also influenced by Confucian thought in the eighteenth century.

For Meiji thinkers, the relationship between Confucianism and Western thought was clear. Amane Nishi explicitly stated, 'Song Confucianism and rationalism, though different in their teachings, are very similar' ('Opening the Gates'). The tradition of Confucianism and Chinese learning in Japan significantly facilitated the integration of Western sociology[7]

THE RECEPTION AND TRANSFORMATION OF SOCIOLOGY IN MEIJI JAPAN

Since the Meiji Restoration, Japan experienced a massive influx of Western culture. The introduction of Western sociology to Japan was just one small part of this broader phenomenon. During this introduction, sociology was positioned upon a foundation of traditional Japanese cultures, including Shinto, Buddhism, Confucianism, and Dutch learning. Meanwhile, there were also contemporary social demands. The birth of Comtean sociology, with its basic principles of progress and order, was a product of the French Revolution and its subsequent turmoil. This parallel holds true for post-Meiji Restoration Japanese society as well. On one side, there was the liberal Freedom and People's Rights Movement aimed at eliminating feudal vestiges of the Edo period, while on the other, there was nation-building by conservative nationalists centered around Emperor Meiji. Both forces absorbed sociological theories that reinforced their respective positions. This led to the introduction not only of advanced French and British sociology but also of emerging German-language sociology. The period from the end of the Meiji era through the Taisho era represents a transition from a phase of sociology's enlightenment to one in which an indigenous Japanese sociology began to be systematized.

NOTES

1. There are exceptional cases like Shoeki Ando (1703–1762), who developed unique radical social criticism without comparing it with Western society.
2. While this insight was gained from knowledge of Western social systems, it could also be seen as a rediscovery of the ideals from the vermilion seal ship trade era. That is, before isolation, in the early Edo period, Japan conducted trade through vermilion seal ships traveling between Japan and Southeast Asia. This involved Confucian natural law ideals and contact with Southeast Asian peoples and their European rulers, where mercantile thought had already begun to emerge.
3. Banzan Kumazawa (1619–1691) during the isolation period also criticized domestic military preparations and warned of threats from foreign peoples.

However, this did not lead to the emergence of modern nationalism. That can be said to have been brought about by the threat of Westerners.

4. A humanistic geographical text written around the sixteenth century that describes the customs of people from different regions of Japan, with a particular focus on samurai ethos and character.

5. 'Auguste Comte once authored five model studies: celestial physics (astronomy), terrestrial physics (physics, chemistry), biology, and sociology' (*Shohakusaiki*). 'This (human studies = sociology) is Comte's creation, derived from the word 'society,' a philosophy discussing the way humans live and nurture each other, encompassing sciences such as politics, law, and religion' ('Seiseihatsuun'), etc.

6. Classification methods of Western learning were known in Japan through the Chinese book *Xixue Fan* by Italian missionary Giulio Aleni (1582–1649), who went to China. It presented a six-fold classification of learning: literature, science, medicine, law, education, and ethics.

7. While earlier Confucianism focused primarily on textual interpretation of classical writings, Song dynasty Confucianism (Zhu Xi's Neo-Confucianism) distinctly differed in that it constructed a systematic worldview by introducing metaphysical concepts such as li (principle) and qi (material force).

CHAPTER 2

The Popularity of Spencer's Evolutionary Sociology: The 1880s

Abstract The rapid development of modern Japanese sociology was prepared by Edo period Confucian scholars, Kokugaku scholars, and Dutch studies scholars. While these individuals' works undoubtedly contained the seeds of sociology, what was more significant was that sociological analysis became absolutely essential during the tumultuous period from the end of the Edo shogunate through the Meiji Restoration. There were expectations that sociology could answer serious questions about how to calm the chaos following the collapse of the old system and what measures needed to be taken to establish a new order.

Looking back at history, Japan established a new government in 1868, replacing the Edo shogunate—the Meiji Restoration. As a result of this major political transformation, reorganizing the national system became an urgent task. To reconstruct politics for establishing a modern nation-state, they needed to study the political systems of Britain, France, and Germany. These were based on academic fields such as political science, state science, and sociology. Western sociological thinkers like Britain's Herbert Spencer (1820–1903), Germany's Lorenz von Stein (1815–1890), and Austria's Ludwig Gumplowicz (1838–1909) were sociologists imported during this trend. Among them, Spencer was the first to capture Japanese interest. The introduction of Spencer's sociology appeared by at least the 1870s. Spencer's first work was *Social Statics* (1851). In Japan, Yukio Ozaki (1858–1954) published it as *Kenri Teiko* in 1877, and Go

© The Author(s), under exclusive license to Springer Nature Switzerland AG 2025
S. Mitupova, K. Yoshino, *Sociology in Japan*, Sociology Transformed, https://doi.org/10.1007/978-3-031-91347-1_2

Matsushima (1854–1940) published it as *Shakai Kenron* in 1881. Both books created a huge response. Furthermore, lecture notes and writings based on Spencer continued to be published in succession:

Homei Hayashi's Social Philosophy (1882)
Tamotsu Sibue's Sociology (1894), Hakubunkan
Kojiro Tatsumi's Lectures on Sociology (1899), Year 11 Advanced
    Religious Studies Lecture Notes from Philosophy Academy

It could be said that the Japanese people's desire for liberal thought and social reform created an extraordinary Spencer boom.

Keywords Social organism theory • Meiji constitution (1889) • Sino-Japanese war (1894–1895) • Russo-Japanese war (1904–1905) • High treason incident (Taigyaku Jiken) • Freedom and people's rights movement (Jiyū Minken Undo) • Auguste Comte • Herbert spencer

TRANSLATION OF THE TERM 'SOCIOLOGY'

When the word 'Sociology' was first introduced to Japan, it was translated as 'Setaigaku' (Study of social manners and customs) or 'Kosairon' (theory of social relations). The translation 'Shakaigaku' began to be used after Shinpachi Seki (1839–1886) translated H. Spencer's *Education: Intellectual, Moral, Physical* (1866) in 1880. Subsequently, when Kotaro Noritake (1860–1909) translated Volume 1 of Spencer's *The Principles of Sociology* (1876), the term 'Shakaigaku' was also adopted for the title. While this translation was published in several installments from 1883, Masami Oishi (1855–1935) simultaneously published his translation of Spencer's *Study of Sociology* (1873) under the title *Shakaigaku*. Through these works, the translation *Shakaigaku* became established in Japan.

Among Spencer's early introducers in Japan, three figures held particularly important positions: Masakazu Toyama (1848–1900), foreign advisor Ernest Francisco Fenollosa (1853–1908), and Nagao Ariga (1860–1921). All three lectured at Tokyo Imperial University.

In the mid-1870s, Toyama studied at the University of Michigan in America, where Spencerian evolutionary sociology was popular at the time. Upon returning to Japan in 1876, he began teaching sociology at Tokyo University (later Tokyo Imperial University). His lectures reportedly consisted of reading excerpts from Spencer's works in English. Students secretly called him 'Spencer's Guardian.' While he is sometimes criticized for not developing his own sociological system, Toyama had other specialized fields, including 'Women in the Age of the Gods' and 'History of Japanese Knowledge and Morality,' collected in his essay collection *Chuzan Sonkou.*

Fenollosa, a foreign advisor teaching philosophy at Tokyo University, similarly introduced Spencer's sociology. His academic approach could be characterized as an attempt to unify evolutionary thought with Hegelian spiritual evolution theory.

Ariga, one of Fenollosa's students, was also greatly influenced by Spencer's evolutionary thought. This is clearly evident in the titles of his three-volume work *Sociology: Theory of Social Evolution* (1883), *Theory of Religious Evolution* (1883), and *Theory of Family System Evolution* (1884).[1] Besides introducing Spencer's theories, he also translated his works. Spencer's theory of evolution from military to industrial society was not unrelated to Japan's situation, as it was transitioning from a samurai-centered feudal system to modern democracy and capitalism. Spencer's arguments were indispensable for Japanese intellectuals of the late nineteenth century in foreseeing their country's future.[2]

However, examining the progression of Ariga's later arguments reveals a gradual shift from Spencer's liberal evolutionary sociology toward centralized state theory, deeply connected to his exposure to Lorenz von Stein's sociology. Stein was also known as an advisor on the Constitution of the Empire of Japan. In 1887, Ariga had the opportunity to directly attend Stein's lectures as an interpreter for Nobuyoshi Kaieda (1832–1906) and Sakura Maruyama (1840–1899) in Vienna. Based on the records of these six months of lectures, Ariga published 'Sutain-shi Kogi' (Lectures of Mr. Stein) in 1889.

In these lectures, Stein does not necessarily discuss sociology systematically. However, they are richly filled with sociological insights about the state. For example, he points out that there are both internal and external factors in obedience to rulers, and various factors that determine a state's strength and weakness. According to Stein, the strength and weakness of a state depend on population density, the development of national spirit and education, and maritime conditions. On the other hand, regarding the desirable state of society, he mentions maintaining class relations while having moderate social mobility. He also noted that there are distinctions between progressive, conservative, and reactionary political positions regarding class and further pointed out that within conservatism, there are two types: those that accept upward and downward social mobility and those that don't.

In this way, Stein's lectures demonstrate sharp sociological analysis. However, what must not be overlooked is that Stein's sociology was a form of Staatslehre (study of the state) that emphasized state governance. Spencer's evolutionary sociology, which advocated freedom and competition, was greatly different in this respect.

From the Meiji Restoration through the Freedom and People's Rights Movement, what was needed to build a modern state centered on the emperor was a sociology for successful state administration. Ariga shifted from progress to order.

NATURAL RIGHTS AND THEIR LIMITATIONS

Natural rights refer to the rights to freedom, equality, and the pursuit of happiness that all humans possess from birth. This concept was also known in mid-Meiji Japan. Hiroyuki Kato (1836–1916), like Nishi and Tsuda, was initially a Western scholar and particularly a pioneer of German studies in Japan. In his early years, he belonged to the Meirokusha[3] and believed in the idealistic rights philosophy of innate human rights theory and the Freedom and People's Rights Movement (civil rights movement). However, after becoming the first president of Tokyo Imperial University in 1877, he withdrew from this view.

From a perspective that faces the reality of a society where individuals are in opposition to each other, the idea of natural rights seemed too idealistic. Kato began to lean toward such critical views of natural rights. One of the sociologists who provided the basis for his argument was the German Austrian sociologist Ludwig Gumplowicz (1838–1909). Gumplowicz emphasized racial struggle in the central process of history from a social Darwinist perspective. Upon encountering this idea, Kato shifted from a natural rights worldview to a social Darwinist worldview. In *The Competition of the Rights of the Strong* (1893), Kato explained the process by which social order is established through struggle and survival of the fittest. In the sense that it accepted the relationship between rulers and ruled and in legitimizing the current ruling class, Kato's sociological thought was compatible with the ideology of Meiji nationalism.[4] This served to check the increasingly radical Freedom and People's Rights Movement.

In the early Meiji period, when liberal democratic thought was being imported into Japan, it was inevitable that Spencer's sociology would become popular. This was true both for those in power and for those who shaped public opinion and formed social movements. Sociology was considered important as a foundation for one's own beliefs.

NOTES

1. Ariga published this work the year after graduating from Tokyo University's Faculty of Letters. It demonstrates his deep understanding and passion for Spencer's sociology. While often viewed as a restatement of Spencer's sociology, there are alternative evaluations: 'Though based on Spencer's theories, it incorporates facts from Japan, China, Korea, and Ainu, and establishes its own theories by incorporating ideas from McLennan, Morgan, and others' (Matsumoto, 1932, p. 4, Shimode, 1932, p. 202). His student Takebe highly praised it: 'Among Meiji era writings on sociology, one must first recommend Nagao Ariga. His three works on social evolution, family system evolution, and religious evolution, even if indebted to Western scholars, remain valuable contributions to academia.'

2. Teccho Suehiro (1849–1896) noted: 'While students enthusiastically discussed the works of Buckle, Guizot, and Mill until five or six years ago, recently this has changed, and works like "Statics" and "Study of Sociology" can be found in every household's study notes, comparable to Wang Chong's Lunheng - truly flourishing indeed.'

3. The Meirokusha was an enlightenment intellectual society formed in early Meiji Japan under the leadership of Mori Arinori after his return from studying in the United States. It was named 'Meiroku-sha' (literally 'Meiji 6 Society') because it was established in 1873, the 6th year of the Meiji era. The society held meetings twice a month and published its own journal called 'Meiroku Zasshi.' From their progressive and pro-Westernization standpoint, they engaged in intellectual discourse across various fields, including society, politics, economics, education, religion, thought, philosophy, and women's issues. They criticized feudalistic thinking and became theoretical advocates for Japan's policy of opening up to the world.

4. Since Kato actually engaged in debates with advocates of people's rights, it is generally believed that he changed his thoughts and stance after the publication of this book.

REFERENCES

Matsumoto, J. (1932). Nihon shakaigaku no enkaku to tenbo [The History and Prospects of Japanese Sociology]. In *Shakaigakusetsu to tenbo [Sociological Theories and Prospects]* (pp. 1–90). (In Japanese).

Shimode, J. (1932). Meiji Shakaigaku Shiryo [Historical Materials of Meiji Sociology]. In *Shimode Junkichi Ikoshu [The Posthumous Manuscripts of Shimode Junkichi]* (pp. 173–233). (In Japanese).

CHAPTER 3

Social Organism Theory: A. Comte and Tongo Takebe

Abstract This chapter deals with the era dominated by social organism theory. In sociology, social organism theory is an approach that analyzes society by comparing it to a living organism where all parts are organically connected and function together. The massive influx of sociology into Japan occurred around 1900, near the end of the Meiji era. Among the various sociological theories introduced during this period, A. Comte's sociology rose to prominence, replacing Spencer, who had dominated the previous era. A distinctive characteristic of Japanese sociology appears in the fact that, contrary to the chronological order of Western sociological history, Spencer's evolutionary sociology became popular first in Japan, followed by the flourishing of Comte's social organism theory. Comte rejected J.J. Rousseau's social contract theory and instead introduced an organismic perspective modeled after biology. Just as biology analyzes the body's structure and functions, Comte divided sociology into social statics (analysis of structure and order) and dynamics (study of development and progress) (H. Spencer also advocated a theory of social evolution where society, as an organism, differentiates and develops from simple to complex forms, similar to biological organisms. In this sense, Spencer was also a supporter of social organism theory.). In Japan, Tongo Takebe became the leading proponent of this organismic sociology.

S. Mitupova, K. Yoshino, *Sociology in Japan*, Sociology Transformed, https://doi.org/10.1007/978-3-031-91347-1_3

Keywords Theory of social organism • A.Comte • Social statics •
Social dynamics • Tongo Takebe

TONGO TAKEBE AND HIS HISTORICAL CONTEXT

In Japan, the Freedom and People's Rights Movement culminated in the
establishment of the Constitution of the Empire of Japan in 1889, followed by the first Imperial Diet in 1890. After winning the Sino-Japanese
War (1894–1895), Japan used the reparations to build ironworks and promote industrialization. As industries developed, labor issues became
increasingly apparent. Against this historical backdrop, during the third
decade of the Meiji era, various sociological theories began flooding into
Japan as if a dam had burst. However, from the perspective of the spread
of liberal thought, this could be seen as moving backward in time. While
Spencer's influence had been overwhelming until recently, this boom
gradually subsided with the Russo-Japanese War (1904–1905) and the
High Treason Incident of 1910. Although sociology was flowing in from
various countries, a trend toward nationalism and Japanism was developing.

Examples include Nobuta Kishimoto's *Sociology* (Meiji 31), introducing Georg Simmel (1858–1918), Momoyo Oka's *Sociology* (Meiji 34)
based on Ludwig Gumplowicz (1838–1909), Wataru Totoki's
(1874–1940) *Summary of Sociology* (Meiji 35) digesting Fairbanks's work,
Ryukichi Endo's *Sociology* (Meiji 36) based on Georges Palante's
(1862–1925) *Precis de sociologie*, and the same author's *Contemporary
Sociology* (Meiji 34) influenced by Giddings. As a late adopter of sociology,
Japan continued to voraciously absorb sociological theories from around
the world, regardless of language or country of origin.[1]

Naturally, there was also extensive translation of major foreign sociological works. During this period, works such as Benjamin Kidd's
(1858–1916) *Social Evolution* (1894), Arthur Fairbanks's (1864–1944)
Introduction to Sociology (1896), Franklin Henry Giddings's (1855–1931)
The Principles of Sociology (1896) and *The Theory of Socialization* (1897),
and Ludwig Gumplowicz's (1838–1909) *Sociologie und Politik* (1892)
were translated into Japanese.

During this period, Takebe's social organism theory was particularly
influential. He taught that society was an organic gathering of people living cooperatively and that the state was an extension of the family.[2] He

based his theory on Auguste Comte. His sociology was built upon a detailed reading and interpretation of Comte's sociology, combined with his unique understanding of Confucianism and political passion.

As Recognized by M.Toyama

Takebe entered the Philosophy Department of Tokyo Imperial University's Faculty of Letters in July 1894. His classmates included several scholars who would later achieve greatness, such as literary critic Chogyū Takayama (1871–1902), religious studies scholar Masaharu Anesaki (1873–1949), and Genyoku Kuwaki (1874–1946). Even among them, his pride stood out remarkably. When his peers or disciples later reminisced about Takebe, they invariably mentioned his bold and uninhibited personality. Anecdotes remain of him frequently boasting that 'Kant, Comte, and Tongo are the three great thinkers' or that 'sociology begins with Comte and reaches its completion with Tongo.'

The year after graduation, in 1897, Takebe published *Riku Sozan*, followed by *Philosophical Overview* the next year. References to sociology and to Spencer, Comte, and Giddings can already be found in these books.

Around the middle of his third year at university, Takebe decided to specialize in sociology under the guidance of Masakazu Toyama. Toyama was the first Japanese person to take up teaching sociology at Tokyo University, working hard to establish sociology lectures there. He had previously participated in the Freedom and People's Rights Movement, joined the new-style poetry movement, and advocated for the abolition of Kanji (Chinese characters). While he was a follower of Spencer, as a sociologist he emphasized empirical specific research rather than being a theorist. Toyama chose Takebe as his successor.

Thus, Takebe came to write his doctoral dissertation in sociology under Toyama. The title was *Comprehensive and Fundamental Research in Sociology*, aiming to construct a grand theoretical system of sociology. In June 1898, after entering graduate school, Takebe was instructed to pursue studies abroad. He first went to Germany and attended the University of Berlin. In June 1900, he left Germany for France. Shortly after, in September, he finished proofreading his doctoral dissertation and submitted it to Tokyo University for review. This dissertation passed the examination in 1902, and he was awarded his doctorate. This dissertation would become his masterwork, *General Sociology* (*Futsu Syakaigaku*), published in four volumes from 1904 to 1919.

Afterward, he visited various parts of Europe, extending his travels to Russia. Looking at his travel essays *Saiyu Manpitsu* (*Western Wandering Notes*), one finds numerous references to the political situations of the countries he visited, indicating his strong interest in political issues. After completing his European tour, Takebe returned home via America in 1901. Immediately after his return in October, he was appointed as a professor.

General Sociology

General Sociology consists of four volumes. Volume 1, published in 1904, is the *Introduction*. It discusses fundamental questions such as 'What is society?' and 'Where are the origins of sociology?' These issues are explored by tracing back to European Greek philosophy and Oriental Confucianism. Volume 2, *Social Physics*, was published in 1905. It discusses specific principles and rules, from general principles like the universe, world, and humanity to elements of society and its emergence and development. Volume 3, concerning *Social Statics*, was published in 1909. It covers everything from the emergence of society to family, state, and international relations and further extends to discussing the functions of economics, social education ('enlightenment'), and politics that serve as the actual driving forces of society. After some time, Volume 4, *Social Dynamics*, was published in 1918, completing the four-volume series spanning almost four years. This final volume focuses on social evolution and civilization.

Takebe's sociological conception is sometimes evaluated as an imitation of Comte's sociology. Indeed, there are numerous elements derived from Comte, such as the distinction between social statics and dynamics, the theory of society as an organism, and the law of three stages of social evolution. Takebe's key concept of 'Jitsuri-shugi'[3] can also be seen as an application of Comte's positivism. In fact, Takebe highly valued Comte. Given this, it's understandable to get the impression that Takebe merely followed Comte. However, upon closer reading of *General Sociology*, this view becomes questionable. This is because at the root of his sociological thinking was not Comte but rather Confucianism. For Takebe, it seems his true intention was to reinforce Confucianism's lack of scientific and realistic recognition with Comte's positivism, attempting to integrate Eastern spirit with Western science.

An outline of this work was published in 1901 in the *Revue internationale de sociologie*, edited by René Worms, under the title *Programme d'une sociologie générale.* Although it was just a table of contents of all four volumes, it provided an opportunity to showcase Japanese sociology's achievements to sociologists worldwide.

Looking back on the history of Japanese sociology, Junichiro Matsumoto evaluated Takebe's *General Sociology* as one of the representative international sociological works of the early twentieth century, likely comparable to the sociological systems of René Worms (1869–1926) and Guillaume de Greef (1842–1924) of that time (Matsumoto, 1947, p. 11).[4]

THE ESTABLISHMENT OF THE JAPANESE INSTITUTE OF SOCIOLOGY

By the Taisho period (1911–1915), Takebe had come to be regarded as the highest authority in Japanese sociology. He also contributed to Japanese sociology at the institutional level through the establishment of the Japanese Institute of Sociology (Nihon Shakaigakuin) in 1913. This was Japan's first nationwide sociological organization. Although Takebe could have established it on his own, he deliberately chose to include Shotaro Yoneda, who was teaching sociology at Kyoto Imperial University, as a collaborator. The following year, in 1914, the organization's journal *Nihon Shakaigakuin Nenpo* (*Annual Report of the Japanese Institute of Sociology*) was launched. This journal continued until 1923, publishing ten volumes before its discontinuation.

There was a specific intention behind Takebe's decision to create this academic society in cooperation with Yoneda. Yoneda was a leading sociologist representing western Japan who had returned from studying in America and France. He had been teaching sociology at Kyoto Imperial University since 1903. Utilizing his natural linguistic abilities, Yoneda was a widely read scholar who introduced foreign sociology to Japan. In Japanese sociological circles, Yoneda was considered, alongside Takebe, to be one of the two pillars leading sociology in eastern and western Japan. By joining forces with Yoneda, Takebe successfully united sociological researchers from across Japan.

Furthermore, it appears Takebe had another intention: to deepen connections with the International Institute of Sociology (Institut international de sociologie) in Paris. Indeed, in 1916, he was elected as a full member of this International Institute of Sociology.

Takebe as a Journalist

Throughout his life, Takebe retained his role as a journalist. He was a prolific writer for the newspaper *Nippon* and magazines such as *Nihonjin* and *Taiyo*, primarily expressing his political views and commentary from his philosophical and sociological perspectives. While at Tokyo University, he associated with Seikyosha's Miyake Setsurei, who managed the magazine *Nihonjin*. In his *Western Wandering Notes*, which can be considered a travel journal from his study abroad, he frequently addressed political and social issues across Europe.

Since 1903, he had been publishing his opinions on international affairs, and particularly amid rising tensions in Japanese-Russian relations, he advocated for war. This manifested in the 'Seven Doctors' Opinion Paper',[5] which urged the government to take a hard-line approach. Among the signatories, Takebe's stance was the most hard-line. When the representative Hirondo Tomizu (1861–1935) was ordered to take a leave of absence, Takebe submitted his resignation to the university. Eventually, he was persuaded to withdraw it and returned to work.

The Russo-Japanese War ended in Japan's victory but also caused significant damage to Japan. Moreover, Japan couldn't obtain war reparations, leading to the Hibiya Riots in 1905. These were public protests against the Portsmouth Peace Treaty, which was signed despite the lack of reparations. How did Takebe react to this? According to him, the post-war social unrest stemmed from Japanese people being poisoned by materialism and individualism. This aligned with the Meiji government's thinking. In 1918, the Meiji Emperor issued the Boshin Imperial Rescript, which advocated international cooperation with Western powers externally and promoted diligence and frugality internally. Takebe promptly responded by writing *Commentary on the Boshin Imperial Rescript* to explain it.

Diligence means hard work, the opposite of laziness. It goes without saying that laziness is the root of national ruin. Frugality means thrift, that is, controlling expenditure according to income, and this is the opposite of luxury. While I hear some shallow economic theories claim that luxury is necessary for civilization, and some even go so far as to say that luxury is the flower of civilization, this is decisively opposed by profound economic theories. There are no examples of economies developing through luxury, no examples of nations prospering without economic development, and no examples of healthy civilization progressing without national prosperity. (Takebe, 1908, p. 99)

Generally, when a country enters war, society naturally tightens under a wartime system. However, after the war, particularly in victorious nations, there tends to be a drift toward frivolity due to a sense of liberation. Warning against this was Takebe's purpose. This thinking wasn't temporary—it remained unchanged through World War I and its aftermath and through the Pacific War. After the war, democratic movements flourished in Japan under the Allied victory, represented by the Taisho Democracy exemplified by Sakuzo Yoshino's 'minponshugi' (democracy). However, even in this era celebrating democracy, Takebe remained wary of excessive individualism and democracy, as seen in his 1920 work 'National Polity, National Policy, and Current Thought Problems.'

> *As long as the individual is considered the ultimate human reality in the universe, even if one doesn't fall into crude, frivolous modern-style democracy, one cannot help but establish lukewarm measures of social solidarity in practice and follow incomplete logic in theory. Only through understanding the unified view of social reality can one grasp the reality of national society as the ultimate human reality, not an illusion, and thereby establish national fundamentalism, which is concrete national society-centered principle based on society-centered thought.* (Takebe, 1920, p. 449)

The kind of society Takebe continuously sought was neither bureaucracy-centered nor people-centered but nation-centered. It was a utopia that merged Comte's social solidarity with Confucian ideals of governing the country and bringing peace to the world. However, in reality, it was also a philosophy that was constantly defeated.

The Generational Shift

We must never forget Takebe's achievements as the first Japanese sociologist to establish his own sociological system and found Japan's first sociological society. Before him, the pinnacle of systematic sociology was Nagao Ariga's 1883 trilogy: *Theory of Social Evolution, Theory of Religious Evolution,* and *Theory of Family System Evolution.* While these works attracted attention when published, they were far less original compared to Takebe's *General Sociology.*

However, by the Taisho period, Takebe's sociological system had come to be viewed as outdated. Instead, the latest sociological theories introduced by Shotaro Yoneda at Kyoto Imperial University were more appealing to the next generation of sociologists. Yasuma Takata, who absorbed Yoneda's theories, wrote *Principles of Sociology* and *Introduction to Sociology*. Eitaro Suzuki, who left Takebe to continue his research under Yoneda, wrote *Principles of Japanese Rural Sociology*. In comparison, sociology at Tokyo Imperial University needed new talent. Teizo Toda, who returned from America and began research in family sociology, took on this role.

NOTES

1. Ryukichi Endo abandoned the social organism theory and advocated psychological sociology under Giddings's influence. This new sociology laid the foundation for Taisho-era sociology. Wataru Totoki worked on systematizing sociology. Because he shifted to criminology as a lecturer at Kyoto Imperial University's Faculty of Letters, his work in sociology did not develop further. The introduction of Gumplowicz's sociology by Kichiji Shinmi (1874–1974) and Momoyo Oka (1874–1945) demonstrates the high level of Japanese sociology during this period.
2. 'Society is an organic human unity of people's cooperative living.' 'The state is an expanded and enlarged form of the family' (General Sociology, Volume 1).
3. 'Jitsuri-shugi' refers to the examination of nature and humanity from both material and spiritual perspectives, aimed at uncovering universal principles that lie beyond scientific thinking.
4. It can be considered one of the representative international sociological works of the early twentieth century. This great work likely stands as a historically significant existence comparable to the systematic works of Worms and de Greef of that time.
5. An opinion paper submitted to the Meiji government by seven doctors, including Tomizu from Tokyo Imperial University's Law Faculty, arguing for the immediate commencement of the Russo-Japanese War (compiled in Koreyasu Kurahara's 1903 *Compilation of Arguments for War with Russia*).

REFERENCES

Matsumoto, J. (1947). *Nihon no Shakaigaku [Japanese Sociology]*. Jichosha. (In Japanese).

Takebe, T. (1901). Programme d'une sociologie générale. *Revue internationale de sociologie*. (In French).

Takebe, T. (1904–1918). *Futsuu Shakaigaku [General Sociology]*. Kinkodo Shoseki. (In Japanese).

Takebe, T. (1908). *Boshin Shosho Engi [Elaboration on the Imperial Rescript of 1908]*. Dobunkan. (In Japanese).

Takebe, T. (1920). *Kokutai Kokuze oyobi Genji no Shiso Mondai [National Polity, National Policy, and Contemporary Ideological Issues]*. Kodokan. (In Japanese).

CHAPTER 4

Sociology and Social Science: Marxism in the Taisho Era (1912–1926)

Abstract This chapter explores the development of 'social science' and 'sociology' in Japanese academic discourse. 'Sociology' was initially established as a distinct discipline, thanks to pioneers like Toyama and Takebe at Tokyo Imperial University. At the same time, 'social science' emerged as a broader framework comprising various disciplines. Initially, sociology in Japan developed its own unique character, blending Western sociological theories (particularly those of Comte and Spencer) with Eastern philosophical traditions, especially Confucianism, as exemplified in Takebe's *General Sociology*. Instead of being viewed as merely a branch of social science or a collection of various social sciences, sociology in Japan established itself as an independent field with its own theoretical foundations and methodological approaches while maintaining dialogue with other social sciences. Within synthetic sociology, it acted as a dominant concept encompassing social sciences. Notably, efforts were made by sociologists to establish 'social science' as a collective term for various disciplines, while it was also referenced in anarchist discussions. Despite being infrequently used as an overarching term, it was employed by Japanese sociologists and social activists, connecting it to the early notion of 'sociology' as a unifying concept. Eventually, 'sociology' was recognized as the leading concept for social sciences in Japan, while 'social science,' particularly in connection with Marxism, gained prominence through the initiatives of the Social Science Society at Tokyo Imperial University.

© The Author(s), under exclusive license to Springer Nature Switzerland AG 2025
S. Mitupova, K. Yoshino, *Sociology in Japan*, Sociology Transformed, https://doi.org/10.1007/978-3-031-91347-1_4

Keywords Taisho era • Sociology • Social sciences • Marxism • Socialist movement • Anarchism

The Emergence and Political Implications of Social Science in Japan

In contemporary discussions, the phrase 'social science' reflects a broad concept encompassing fields like sociology, economics, political science, and law. The Japanese equivalent of 'social science' only emerged in the early 1920s, being an obscure term. At that time, the notion of 'social science' was closely aligned with Marxism rather than merely serving as an overarching term for disciplines such as sociology. This association arose because the establishment of the Social Science Research Association in 1923 significantly contributed to the term's adoption in Japan, with Marxism underpinning its perspective on societal issues. The Social Science Research Association functioned not just as a Marxist research body but also as a hub for radical political movements. Consequently, the term 'social sciences,' as it gained traction, essentially became another label for Marxism rather than a broader category. The term 'social science' appeared within the realm of Japanese sociology. For instance, sociologist Shotaro Yoneda employed the phrase 'social science' during a lecture in 1906, categorizing economics, national studies, religious studies, and law as components of social science. (Yoneda, 1906). Additionally, anarchist Sakae Osugi referenced 'social science' in a 1915 essay, asserting that individuals must strictly adhere to the teachings of the state. He remarked that in the realm of social sciences—including political science, law, economics, and history—there is little room for personal interpretation beyond state-approved narratives. Osugi (1916) used 'social science' in this comprehensive manner multiple times, despite not being recognized as a conventional 'intellectual.'

'Social Science' in the History of Japanese Sociology

In 1930, Kaname Hayashi included the term 'social science' in his *Dictionary of Social Science*, where he noted that it was often associated with a specific interpretation, particularly Marxism, within the context of the student social science movement. However, he emphasized that this interpretation does not represent a comprehensive definition of 'social science.' He further remarked that while 'social science' is frequently perceived as equivalent to sociology, it actually serves as a broad term encompassing various disciplines that examine social phenomena, distinguishing them from the natural sciences. (Hayashi, 1930, p. 479). In the 1944 *Dictionary of Sociology*, Shinmei discussed 'social science' and pointed out that sociology is often used interchangeably with this term. He noted that sociology, particularly when framed within a synthetic sociological framework, tends to incorporate various specialized social sciences into its structure, thereby blurring the lines between sociology and social science. Shinmei argued that within the realm of synthetic sociology, the terms 'social science' and 'sociology' are indistinguishable. This approach seeks to achieve a holistic understanding of society, with figures like Comte and Spencer viewed as key representatives of this ideology.

A notable figure in the establishment of a systematic approach to sociology leading up to 1923 was Takebe Tongo. Takebe, the founder of the Japan Sociological Institute, was significantly influenced by Comte's all-encompassing sociology. The synthetic sociology exemplified by Takebe dominated the sociological landscape. Thus, Hayashi's critical remarks about the term 'not being a general principle' refer to the synthetic sociology that conflates social science with sociology.

In these critiques, the term 'social science' was employed as a broad concept to encompass various social disciplines. One notable critic of synthetic sociology was Takayoshi Endo. In his 1901 work, Genshi-Kinzai Sociology, Endo expressed his views on the subject, stating, 'The voice of sociology resonates in numerous forms today.' He noted that while sociology is celebrated by many, if it were merely an aggregation of social sciences, it would not hold much significance. According to Endo, it is only through the theory of collective consciousness that sociology can establish itself as an independent discipline. At that time, it was the synthetic sociology proposed by Takebe and others that viewed sociology as 'merely a collection of various social sciences.'

Shotaro Yoneda's lecture collection, titled *Gendai no Shakaigaku* (Yoneda, 1906 *Contemporary Sociology*), frequently mentions 'social science' and 'social sciences.' In a chapter called *The Essence of Social Studies*, he categorizes social studies into two main areas: 'social theory' and 'social practice,' with 'social philosophy' and 'social science' falling under the first category. Yoneda describes social science as the examination of specific aspects of social reality, including fields such as economics, law, religion, and government. He asserts that economics, political science, religious studies, and legal studies are all considered social sciences.

References to these ideas appear in Yoneda's later works, *Theory of Sociology* (1913) and *Critique and Establishment of the Idea of Sociology* (1914). Takata Yasuma, influenced by Yoneda, wrote a paper titled *Sociology and Social Science* during the years 1917 to 1918. He examined the interplay between 'sociology' and 'social science' and sought to define 'sociology as a distinct social science,' where social science serves as the overarching category and sociology as a subset. It is essential to recognize that all these developments occurred prior to 1923. From the sociological context leading up to 1923, two key observations can be made. First, the synthetic sociology that was prominent from the late nineteenth century through the 1920s did not refer to 'social science' as a broad, overarching concept as understood today; instead, it relied on the term 'sociology.' Second, before 1923, sociologists who were critical of synthetic sociology endeavored to establish sociology as an independent discipline, using the term 'social science' as a broader category in this effort.

SAKAE OSUGI'S SOCIAL SCIENCE

Sakae Osugi disputes this perspective, having been deeply influenced by anarcho-syndicalism, which he actively promoted within the context of Japanese social movements. His involvement with anarcho-syndicalism began around 1906, emphasizing labor union principles. In 1913, he established the first Syndicalism Study Group. Interestingly, Osugi mentioned 'social science' in the journal *Kindai Shiso* (Modern Thought) as early as 1912. Having lost many friends during these upheavals, including Koutoku Akisui in the Daigyakuten incident in 1910, Osugi utilized this publication, along with others like *Heimin Shinbun* (Common People's Newspaper), to advance his anti-government stance. His writings, including *Instinct and Creation* and *Tendencies of Modern Science*, were pivotal in shaping anti-government discourse at that time. In *Tendencies of Modern Science*, Osugi draws a connection between 'social science' and 'natural science,' likening it to disciplines such as physics and astronomy. He critiques the use of modern scientific methods across various fields, including history, law, economics, and political science, and continues to apply the term 'social science' broadly in his 1915 work. His use of this term can be traced to two primary influences: first, his exposure to contemporary Japanese sociologists, including Takayoshi Endo, and his recognition of

Yoneda as a significant figure in Japanese sociology. However, this influence alone does not fully clarify his terminology.

Osugi viewed social sciences as inclusive of 'historiography,' a classification absent in the works of Endo and Yoneda, whom he seemingly studied. Notably, his 1912 article, *Tendencies of Modern Science*, is largely a summarized interpretation of Kropotkin's theories. A comparison reveals that this piece closely mirrors Kropotkin's, 1894 lecture, *The New Age* (Kropotkin, 1894). Additionally, Kropotkin discusses 'social science' in other writings, such as his 1901 essay on modern science and anarchism. He argues that employing natural science methods to analyze economic phenomena exposes the so-called laws of bourgeois social sciences, including political economy, as unfounded claims rather than true laws. Kropotkin stresses that these alleged 'laws' lack empirical validation, emphasizing the need for rigorous examination (Kropotkin, 1894).

Bakunin, a prominent anarchist like Kropotkin, shares a critical perspective on the scientific 'laws' of his time. He critiques historical science for its tendency to abstract events, thereby neglecting the realities of people's lives, as noted in his 1882 work *The Whip's German Empire and the Social Revolution*. Bakunin argues that true historical science does not yet exist and that understanding its complex nature is challenging. He believes that if such a science were to evolve, it would simply reflect the material and ideological conditions of society without addressing the needs of the many, prioritizing the interests of a few instead. Bakunin refers to this concept as 'social science,' highlighting its shortcomings in representing the broader population.

Bakunin questioned the appropriateness of criticizing historical science, suggesting that such criticism would be both unwise and harsh. He argued that the essence of an individual cannot be fully encapsulated by ideas, reflections, or language, which only convey abstract concepts. He pointed out that just as individuals are difficult to comprehend in the present, they were equally elusive in the past. Therefore, he concluded that social science, envisioned as the science of the future, would inevitably overlook individual experiences (Bakounine, 1882). Osugi viewed Bakunin's insights on history as 'a broad and clear perspective on the philosophy of history' (Osugi, 1920). His classification of 'historiography' within social science stems from his engagement with the anarchist notions of figures like Kropotkin and Bakunin. From this discussion, two key points emerge. First, prior to 1923, Osugi employed 'social science' as an overarching term to encompass various social sciences. Second, his concept of 'social science' was influenced by anarchist discourse.

The Evolution and Suppression of 'Social Science'

Firstly, 'sociology' emerged as the central concept within synthetic sociology. Secondly, before 1923, sociologists aimed to establish 'social science' as a unifying term across various disciplines. Lastly, Sakae Osugi's use of 'social science' was deeply rooted in anarchist discourse. Evidence suggests that Japanese sociologists and social activists did utilize it to some degree, linking it to the early adoption of 'sociology' as a comprehensive concept. By that time, 'sociology' had already gained prominence as the leading framework for social sciences in Japan, with figures like Endo, Yoneda, and Takata striving to elevate 'social science' to a similar status. The withdrawal of Takebe, a supporter of synthetic sociology, just before 1923 marked a significant shift, allowing 'social science,' particularly associated with Marxism, to take the lead in the field. This raises further questions about whether 'social science' circulated solely through its Marxist connections, necessitating an examination of the activities of sociologists influenced by anarchism. Notably, Yoneda's early use of 'social science' in lectures and publications, along with the contributions of Endo and Takata, underscores the diverse influences shaping the discourse around social sciences during this period.

Sakae Osugi was influenced by the works of sociologists Endo and Yoneda, as well as by the anarchist ideas of figures like Kropotkin and Bakunin. Osugi's contributions and those of anarchists are noteworthy; the inaugural issue of *Kindai Shiso* published by him in 1912, garnered considerable attention and attracted many notable contributors, gaining popularity in literary circles. *The Heimin Shinbun* (Common People's Newspaper), which began publication in 1914 following *Kindai Shiso*, faced severe restrictions, with five out of six issues banned. Government surveillance stifled the activities of Osugi and his peers, extending even to university administrations. In 1928, a more aggressive crackdown on the Newcomers' Association and social science groups at Tokyo Imperial University began, targeting Marxist interpretations of 'social science.' This repression likely contributed to the dominance of the 'social sciences' and heralded a decline in societal discourse.

REFERENCES

Bakounine, M. (1882–1981). *L'Empire Knouot-Germanique et la Révolution Sociale, Novemre 1870–Avril 1871.* Archives Bakounine = Bakunin-Archiv, VII, E.J. Brill, 1–192. (In French).

Hayashi, K. (1930). Social Science. In S. Shisosha (Ed.), *Shakai Kagaku Daijiten [Dictionary of Social Science]* (pp. 479–480). Kaizosha. (In Japanese).

Kropotkin, P. (1894). *Les Temps Nouveaux. Au Bureau de La Revolte* (Japanese Translation by Ishikawa, S. (1929)). *Atarashiki Jidai.* Shunyodo.

Osugi, S. (1916). Kojinteki Shisaku [Personal Thought]. In *Roudo Undo no Tetsugaku.* Toundo Shokan. (In Japanese).

Osugi, S. (1920). *Kropotkin Kenkyu [Kropotkin Study].* Arusu. (In Japanese).

Yoneda, S. (1906). *Genzai no Shakaigaku [Contemporary Sociology].* Okayama Prefectural Education Association. (In Japanese).

CHAPTER 5

Psychological Sociology in the Taisho Era: Shorato Yoneda's Introduction of F. Giddings and G. Tarde

Abstract Yoneda Shotaro was a sociologist who was active primarily at Kyoto Imperial University from the Meiji era through the pre-war Showa period. Along with Takebe Tongo, he is known as one of the fathers of Japanese sociology. His diverse sociological research is easily apparent through his numerous publications of books and papers on sociology and social philosophy. Like other sociologists of this period, Yoneda can be characterized as an enlightenment scholar. However, in contrast to his prolific output, there are surprisingly few works where he systematically presented his own theoretical framework. If pressed to name one, we could point to *Theory of Sociology* published in the first and second issues of volume 1 of the *Annual Report of the Japanese Institute of Sociology* in December 1913 (Taisho 2). Additionally, in *Modern Sociological Theory*, a collection of Yoneda's posthumous works edited by his students Takata Yasuma and Usui Jisyo, there are several chapters that provide insight into his sociological framework. However, these do not present the complete sociological system he had envisioned during his lifetime. Therefore, to understand Yoneda's sociological framework, readers must undertake the task of reconstructing it from his writings throughout his life. In this chapter, we aim to reconstruct the height of Japanese sociology from the late Meiji to Taisho periods by presenting Yoneda Shotaro's sociological framework.

© The Author(s), under exclusive license to Springer Nature
Switzerland AG 2025
S. Mitupova, K. Yoshino, *Sociology in Japan*, Sociology
Transformed, https://doi.org/10.1007/978-3-031-91347-1_5

Keywords Pure sociology (Junsei Shakaigaku) • synthetic sociology (Sogo Shakaigaku) • Mutual interaction (Sogo Sayo) • Theory of social evolution (Shakai Shinkaron) • Social epistemology (Shakai Chishikigaku)

YONEDA'S 'PURE SOCIOLOGY' AND JAPANESE SOCIOLOGY IN THE TAISHO ERA

In September 1907 (Meiji 40), Yoneda was appointed to teach sociology at the newly established Faculty of Letters at Kyoto Imperial University. This was a promotion from his previous position teaching sociology at Doshisha University. At Kyoto Imperial University, Yoneda served until March 1925 (Taisho 14). While he taught various specialized courses at the university, he notably lectured on 'Introduction to Pure Sociology' as a required course for all students.[1]

Yoneda was reluctant in discussing his own sociological framework. Why was this the case? One reason may be that Yoneda prioritized pursuing unknown knowledge rather than organizing existing knowledge. This approach was particularly valuable for Japanese sociologists of the time who were trying to catch up with Western sociology.

Shortly before retiring from Kyoto University, Yoneda began preparing to publish his sociological framework at the request of a publisher. While he had completed a significant portion of the manuscript, he unfortunately passed away before it could be published.[2] Therefore, to understand Yoneda's conceived sociological framework, one must reconstruct it by gathering relevant elements from the vast materials he left behind.

When was Yoneda's concept of 'Pure Sociology' formed? It first appeared in *Contemporary Sociology*, published in April 1906 (Meiji 39). This book was a record of lectures hosted by the Okayama Prefecture Education Association the previous year. Unusually for Yoneda, who didn't leave behind his own systematic sociological framework, we can find descriptions of his sociological perspective in this work. Through analyzing *Contemporary Sociology*, we will examine how Yoneda acquired the idea of 'Pure Sociology' and how he developed it. This is important because it formed one of the streams of Japanese sociology after the Taisho era, specifically the genealogy of psychological sociology.

LESSONS FROM GIDDINGS

After graduating from Nara English School in 1891, Yoneda traveled to America with his missionary teacher and entered the seminary. He then went on to focus on studying sociology under Giddings at Columbia University. Since his time at Nara English School, Yoneda had been interested in anthropology.[3] His move toward studying sociology, a related science, likely stemmed from this empirical interest. At Columbia University, Yoneda devoted his energy to reading extensively across various fields. F. Giddings (1855–1931) had published *The Theory of Sociology* (1894) and *The Principles of Sociology* (1896) during this period.

In *The Theory of Sociology* (1894), Giddings posed the question: 'Are there certain essential facts, causes or laws in society, which are common to communities of all kinds, at all times, and which underlie and explain the more special social form?' He answered 'Yes' and explained as follows: Sociology is 'the science of social elements and first principles. It is not the inclusive, but the fundamental social science. It is not the sum of the social sciences, but the groundwork, in which they find a common basis.' This was precisely when heated debates about the nature and scope of sociology were taking place in America.

Notably, Giddings went further by referring to Gabriel Tarde's *Les lois de l'imitation* (*The Laws of Imitation*), stating that 'in suggestion and imitation we have, beyond any doubt, those most primary, most elementary, social facts, for which we have been looking. They are the phenomena that differentiate association, in the true or social sense, from mere physical association or concours.' Giddings clearly found sociology's subject matter in Tarde's concept of 'imitation.'

Of course, Giddings didn't accept Tarde's theory wholesale. In his subsequent work *Principles of Sociology*, he criticized Tarde's concept of imitation as being too general. Giddings reached his own conclusion that 'this consciousness of kind is the elementary, the generic social fact.' Thus, he established that seeking this 'consciousness of kind' was sociology's purpose. Giddings believed this provided sociology with its own distinct domain separate from other social sciences.

Yoneda had the opportunity to learn directly from Giddings when these works were being published. He learned that Giddings's concepts of primary or elementary social facts, and particularly the idea of consciousness of kind, were developed through a critical examination of Tarde's laws of imitation. Consequently, in 1900 (Meiji 22), Yoneda left Giddings at

Columbia University and went to Paris to study under Tarde, who was a professor at the Collège de France. How did Yoneda view the relationship between Tarde and Giddings?

> *At one time, I [Yoneda] also strongly endorsed Tarde's theory, believing that his imitation theory best demonstrated the fundamental characteristics of social phenomena. In fact, I went to study in France specifically to research his theories more deeply under Tarde's direct guidance. However, as I studied further, I began to feel dissatisfied with certain aspects of Tarde's imitation theory. I was particularly influenced by the criticisms made by my mentor, the renowned American sociologist Giddings.* (Yoneda, 1906, p. 112)

After criticizing Tarde's imitation theory, Giddings advanced the argument that consciousness of kind was society's 'most primary, most elementary, social facts.' However, as is well known, Giddings's concept of consciousness of kind faced various criticisms from other sociologists. This led Giddings to deepen his thoughts on consciousness, developing the idea of 'stimulus and response' processes. On the one hand, stimulus produces favorable responses, which is imitation. On the other hand, different responses like antipathy and opposition can occur. Therefore, Giddings felt the need to capture not only the formation of 'consciousness of kind' underlying imitation but also aspects of opposition. This led him to focus on the more fundamental psychological state of stimulus and response.

Thus, Giddings came to view society as a combination of stimulus and response. However, despite reaching this point, he didn't make these the main research subjects of sociology or develop them methodologically as a branch of sociology. Yoneda felt dissatisfied with Giddings in this regard. In contrast, Tarde showed a strong interest in sociological methodology. This background led to Yoneda's decision to study under Tarde.

CRITICAL ACCEPTANCE OF G. TARDE'S THEORY OF IMITATION

Tarde's sociology emerged as a critique of evolutionism (represented by Comte and Spencer) and the then-dominant biological sociology. His position was based on psychologism and non-historicism, standing in direct opposition to the biological sociology prevalent in the sociological community at that time.

Tarde first addressed the question of what it means to be 'scientific' (savant), explaining as follows. Generally, the purpose of science is to clarify causal relationships. This is indisputable. However, causal relationships alone are not the only objects of science. More important is the infinite repetition of these causal relationships. According to Tarde, science's task is to quantitatively grasp the infinite repetition of phenomena—in other words, to reveal their universality.

However, when observing phenomena, there are both universal and particular aspects. One might even say that particular aspects are more common. These are what we call one-time historical facts. Among these, the aspect that Tarde believed sociology should deal with was not the particular aspects of phenomena but rather the infinitely repeating aspects of social phenomena. In other words, sociology's purpose is to discover what is 'purely social' (purement social) in phenomena. From this perspective, Tarde identified 'imitation' as the infinitely repeating social fact. He argued that imitation is something that repeats infinitely in human phenomena, and therefore the laws of imitation can be applied to all social phenomena—past, present, or potential—making them the most universal and general. He considered this repetitive phenomenon to be the most typical form of all universal phenomena, referring to it as 'all social, biological, or physical repetition' or 'the most striking and most typical forms of universal repetition' (formes les plus frappantes et le plus typiques). Social repetition is imitation, and therefore sociology as a science studies the laws of imitation. Thus, the 'laws of imitation' became central to his sociology. Tarde called this type of sociology pure and abstract sociology (sociologie pure et abstraite) or general sociology (sociologie générale).[4]

The term 'pure sociology' inherited this sociological perspective from Tarde. However, its content was not identical to Tarde's. In his posthumous work *Modern Sociological Theories*, Yoneda described his differences from Tarde as follows:

> *I was earliest and most sincerely drawn to Tarde's sociology. (This wasn't solely for academic reasons; my circumstances and mental state when I began studying sociology in America played no small part). However, I wasn't blindly following Tarde from the beginning. I developed the concept of interaction between minds differently. Also, in the approach to establishing pure sociology, I differed from Tarde. While fundamentally accepting Tarde's concept of pure sociology, I found many unsatisfactory points in its practical development. In particular, I felt dissatisfied that Tarde's sociology lacked synthetic sociology. Thus, I came*

to believe that Comte and Mill's concept of synthetic sociology needed to be puri-
fied through the concept of pure sociology, and conversely, that Tarde's concept of
pure sociology needed to be purified through the concept of synthetic sociology.
(Yoneda, 1948)

THE CONCEPTION OF PURE SOCIOLOGY

After spending two years in France, Yoneda returned to Japan in 1902 (Meiji 35) and began teaching sociology at Doshisha University. While the exact content of his lectures from that time is unknown, we can imagine that it was similar to his 1906 (Meiji 39) work, *Contemporary Sociology*. The table of contents of this book is as follows:

Lecture 1: The Possibility of Sociological Study
Lecture 2: The Essence and Possibility of Sociology
Lectures 3 and 4: Methods of Sociological Research
Lecture 5: The True Nature of Social Phenomena and the Substance of Society

The sociology presented in this book is not necessarily systematic. However, we can identify the conception of Yoneda's later sociological system, particularly his pure sociology. Through careful reading of this book, we can understand how Yoneda attempted to construct his own sociological system based on the fundamental ideas of Giddings and Tarde while also drawing from many other sociological theories. His central question can be summarized as follows: What should be the true object of sociology?

According to Yoneda, the true object of sociology should be 'the true nature of social phenomena or the substance of society.' According to Comte, the gradual and continuous influence of generations was the characteristic of society, and this intergenerational relationship was the distinctive quality of social phenomena.

However, Yoneda pursued this further, noting that Comte's concept of gradual and continuous generational influence still left unclear points. Yoneda thought that Comte had not clarified how one era receives influence from another—that is, how the present is influenced by the past and affects the future. This is where Italian sociologist Icilio Vanni (1855–1903) becomes relevant. Vanni, along with Alessandro Groppali (1874–1959) and others, was a sociologist who contributed to establishing the foundational theories during the formative period of Italian sociology. Yoneda had already shown a deep interest in Italian sociology during his stay in America.

Vanni argued that as society evolves, social products become stimuli for an era and causes of creation, thereby becoming the driving force and mechanism for the evolution of later eras. According to Yoneda, Comte's characterization of social phenomena was made significantly more precise by Vanni.

Furthermore, Vanni was one of the first scholars to clearly and properly understand the relationship between sociology and social sciences. He divided sociology into three aspects. The first branch synthesizes social science research to explain society as a whole. The second branch provides an overview of society as a whole to determine the direction and research domains for each social science. The third branch presents methodology and classification for social sciences.

While social sciences study parts of society, sociology studies how their theories relate to society and how they change when incorporated into society. This perspective of Vanni provided significant inspiration for the formation of Yoneda's sociology.

Psychological Sociology

The trend in sociology at the beginning of the twentieth century shifted from rationalism to psychologism. Le Bon, Tarde, and Durkheim were among the first to introduce this intellectual current to sociology. Durkheim believed that social facts exist outside of individuals and exert pressure on them from the outside. However, he failed to explain how social facts emerge and establish themselves, ultimately falling into a kind of metaphysics. In contrast, Tarde identified imitation as the distinctive characteristic of social facts. Yet upon closer examination, not all social phenomena arise from imitation, nor does imitation necessarily generate social phenomena. Imitation cannot be the most basic characteristic of elementary social phenomena. There must be a purer characteristic—and it was Giddings who discovered this.

Giddings started with Tarde's theory of imitation and criticized it. As a result, he demonstrated that not all imitation necessarily creates social relationships and that the foundation for social relationships is not imitation but rather the consciousness of belonging to the same kind—the consciousness of kind theory.

For Giddings, '*Society, in the original meaning of the word, is companionship, converse, association, and all true social facts are psychical in their nature*' (Giddings, 1896, p. 3). In seeking the simplest social fact that establishes society, Giddings arrived at the fact of stimulus and response. '*The cultural setting is at every stage of its evolution a product of antecedent reactions. It is, therefore, a consequence partly of reactions to primary stimuli and partly of compounded effects of reactions to previous secondary stimuli. The ingredients thus become inextricably entangled.*'

However, Yoneda's sociological perspective included conflict theories from Gumplowicz and Novicow and the sociology of imitation or coercion from Tarde and Durkheim. When he tried to comprehend these ideas in the most general and abstract way possible, Yoneda arrived at the concept of 'mutual interaction between the minds of two or more individuals.' This became the foundational idea of Yoneda's pure sociology. While *Contemporary Sociology* mentions Tarde's sociologie pure, it does not yet present the content of Yoneda's own pure sociology. However, it does show the point that Yoneda's sociology had reached at that time.

According to this work, it is divided into Part One: Social Epistemology and Part Two: Social Principles. Part Two is further divided into Section One: Theory of Social Existence, Section Two: Theory of Social Evolution, and Section Three: Theory of Social Laws.

Part 1: Social Epistemology (Shakai Chishiki Gaku)

Section 1: The Nature of Social Knowledge
Section 2: Methods of Social Research
Section 3: The Substance of Society, True Nature of Social Phenomena, and Their Classification
Section 4: The System of Social Sciences
Section 5: Historical Development of Social Sciences

Part Two: Principles of Social Science (Shakai Genri Gaku)

Section 1: Theory of Social Existence

Class 1: Formation of Society
Class 2: Social Structure and Operation
Class 3: Types of Society
Class 4: Types of Personality

Section 2: Theory of Social Evolution

Class 1: Driving Forces of Social Evolution
Class 2: Process of Social Evolution
Class 3: Classes of Social Evolution
Class 4: Destination of Social Evolution and Social Progress

Section 3: Theory of Social Laws

Chapter 1: Relationship and Summary of Various Social Laws
Chapter 2: Relationship Between Social Laws and Other Laws

Among these sections, Part One, Section Three, 'The Substance of Society, True Nature of Social Phenomena, and Their Classification' and Part Two, Section One, 'Theory of Social Existence' correspond in content to what would later become pure sociology. Additionally, Part Two, Section Two 'Theory of Social Evolution' overlaps with later synthetic sociology, while Section Three 'Theory of Social Laws' and most of Part One 'Social Epistemology' likely correspond to what Yoneda called 'organizational sociology.'

Viewed this way, it becomes clear that Yoneda had already organized his thoughts to some extent regarding sociology's subject matter and scope, and the conceptual definition of society or social phenomena before his appointment at Kyoto University. And it's evident that pure sociology was fundamental to this organization.

Yoneda's conception of pure sociology shares many similarities with Leopold von Wiese's (1876–1969) concept of social relations. However, Wiese first published his formal sociological ideas in a 1920 paper in Schmollers Jahrbuch (von Wiese, 1920). Therefore, Yoneda conceived his pure sociology independently of, and prior to, Wiese.

Yoneda was appointed to Kyoto University in September 1907 (Meiji 40). It was around this time that he systematized his pure sociology. Reflecting on Yoneda's lectures from that period, Takata Yasuma noted that in 1907 (Meiji 40), the theme was 'History of Sociology,' and the following year it was 'Introduction to Sociology.'

In my [Yoneda's] *sociological system established around 1908–9, the concept of pure sociology, which I recognized as the central branch, originated from Tarde's perspective. However, it was also constructed by critically incorporating Simmel's views.*

The first point to note when considering Yoneda's sociological system is that pure sociology was not the entirety of his sociological system. His *Theory of Sociology* is presented in volumes 1 and 2 of Nihon Shakaigakuin Nenpo (The Annals of the Japanese Institute of Sociology).

Division 1: Systemative sociology or directive sociology
Division 2: Pure sociology or societics
Division 3: Synthetic sociology or societology

The term 'directive sociology' in Division 1 likely follows Vanni's terminology. It is responsible for organizing and arranging theoretical research about society. Division 2 corresponds to the realist aspect of sociology. It is divided into abstract and concrete aspects. The abstract portion is pure sociology, which deals with what are called the fundamental facts of social phenomena or minimal, ultimate, irreducible facts. Pure sociology captures the essence of such social reality and studies it in abstraction from all additional facts. Division 3, synthetic sociology, studies concrete facts formed by the addition and combination of various facts to this essence.

Among these, the fundamental fact of social phenomena identified as the object of pure sociology is the mutual relationship or interaction between minds. In other words, Yoneda's pure sociology studies the principles of the fundamental fact of social phenomena—the mutual relationship or interaction between minds—in abstraction from all other facts.

DEVELOPMENT FROM PURE TO SYNTHETIC SOCIOLOGY

Yoneda's sociological concepts remained fundamentally unchanged throughout his life. Rather, they were only examined and expanded through the methodologies of numerous scholars of his time, including Wilhelm Dilthey (1833–1911), Max Weber (1864–1920), Max Scheler (1874–1928), and Ernst Troeltsch (1865–1923). For Yoneda, his ultimate understanding was that sociology is the science of universal understanding of social reality. Pure sociology lies on one side, while synthetic sociology lies on the other. The former studies the interactions and interrelationships between minds to investigate the foundations of social reality. The latter, based on pure sociology, organizes knowledge of social phenomena as a whole by synthesizing the findings of specialized social sciences.

How does synthetic sociology, grounded in pure sociology, develop? While Yoneda certainly attempted to demonstrate this through numerous works, he left no systematic writings to explain it, only a vague overall picture. However, there is no doubt that by the 1920s (Taisho era), Yoneda had eliminated philosophical elements from sociology, rejected the class nature of sociology, and established sociology as a science. In this sense, it can be said that Yoneda dramatically advanced Japanese sociology.

NOTES

1. According to Isamu Donao, who entered Kyoto University in 1914 (Taisho 3), though details are unclear, Yoneda reportedly gave a lecture on 'synthetic sociology' shortly after his appointment.
2. His official reason for retirement was stated to be the completion of *System of Sociology*, and advertisements for it had even appeared in *Kaizo* magazine.
3. He wrote an article titled 'Amatori-bune' in the magazine *Geibun*, discussing the relationship between sun worship and birds. This demonstrates Yoneda's interest in empirically analyzing religious and anthropological facts.
4. While Ward had *Pure Sociology* (1903) and Small had *General Sociology* (1905), Ward's use of 'pure' was vaguely theoretical in contrast to 'applied,' and Small's 'general' meant synthetic. Although the names were identical, their logical and methodological structures were fundamentally different from Tarde's.

REFERENCES

Giddings, F. H. (1896). *The Principles of Sociology*. Macmillan & Co.

von Wiese, L. (1920). Die Soziologie als Einzelwissenschaft. Schmollers Jahrbuch für Gesetzgebung. *Verwaltung und Volkswirtschaft im Deutschen Reich, 44*(2), 31–51.

Yoneda, S. (1906). Contemporary Sociology. Okayama Prefecture Private Education Association. *Genkon no shakaigaku*. (In Japanese).

Yoneda, S. (1948). *Bankin shakaigaku ron [Modern Sociological Theory]*. Kan Shoin. (In Japanese).

CHAPTER 6

Exploring Ethnicity Through Sociology in Showa Japan: Takata Yasuma's 'Total Society'

Abstract The Taisho era (1911–1926) in Japan was a period marked by the penetration of mass culture and democracy. Thanks to the efforts of scholars like Takebe and Yoneda from the Meiji period, sociology was striving to catch up with international standards. In the global academic sphere of sociology, attempts were being made to address the following fundamental questions: What is the distinct subject matter of sociology? How should sociology be positioned among other social sciences? What exactly constitutes sociology? Yoneda categorized these issues into three types of sociology: organizational sociology, pure sociology, and synthetic sociology. The person who applied this to the analysis of actual society was Yasuma Takata, whom we will discuss in this chapter. Takata systematized these three fields of sociology—organizational sociology, pure sociology, and synthetic sociology—as defined by Yoneda and compiled them into a major work titled *Shakaigaku Genri* (*Principles of Sociology*). This achieved the long-cherished ambition of Japanese sociology to complete a comprehensive sociological system. Subsequently, Takata developed his ethnic theory by applying this sociology to practical issues. This meant that Japanese sociology had achieved the integration of pure theory (pure sociology) with a comprehensive understanding of real-world problems (synthetic sociology).

Keywords Association (Ketugou) • Partial society (Bubun Shakai) • Total society (Zentai Syakai) • Broad ethnicism (Kou Minzokusyugi) • Ethnic harmony (Minzoku Kyouwa) • Desire for group living (Gunkyo no Yokubou) • Desire for power (Chikara no Yokubou)

TAKATA YASUMA'S EARLY MASTERWORK, *THE PRINCIPLES OF SOCIOLOGY* (1919)

The subject matter of sociology is the interaction between minds. In society, people can develop both friendly feelings and antagonistic emotions toward each other. Moreover, these feelings can intersect within the same individual. Why does this occur? Takata explained this through two emotions inherent in humans: 'the desire for group living' and 'the desire for power.' The former is similar to Giddings's consciousness of kind. The latter resembles Friedrich Nietzsche's (1844–1900) ideas but can be rephrased as self-interest or desire for power. These correspond respectively to what Tönnies of the same era defined as essential will and arbitrary will.

Because these desires coexist within an individual's consciousness, people may develop competitive or antagonistic feelings toward previously friendly companions when triggered by certain circumstances. The same applies to society. Society is not built solely on the unity of homogeneous members. Not everyone supports society's central values; some sharply criticize them. However, Takata's view of society is that this tension serves as the driving force that propels society forward.

The table of contents of *Principles of Sociology* is as follows:

Part 1: Sociology
>   Chapter 1: The Concept of Sociology/Chapter 2: Problems of Sociology
>   Chapter 3: Theory of Social Essence/Chapter 4: Principles of Social Constitution

Part 2: Theory of Social Formation
>   Chapter 1: General Theory/Chapter 2: Theory of Homogeneous Association
>   Chapter 3: Theory of Heterogeneous Association/Chapter 4: Theory of Social Consciousness

Part 3: Theory of Social Forms
> Chapter 1: General Theory/Chapter 2: Abstract Forms/Chapter 3:
>> Concrete Forms
> Chapter 4: Direct Society/Chapter 5: Direct–Indirect Society
> Chapter 6: Indirect–Direct Society/Chapter 7: Indirect Society
> Chapter 8: Social Spheres and Social Relations/Chapter 9: Static
>> Interrelations of Social Forms
> Chapter 10: Dynamic Interrelations Between Social Forms—
>> Trends of Change
> Chapter 11: Explanation of Dynamic Interrelations

Part 4: Theory of Social Consequences
> Chapter 1: General Theory/Chapter 2: Development of Culture/
> Chapter 3: Development of Freedom
> Chapter 4: Development of Individuality/Chapter 5: Conclusion.
>> (Takata, 1919)

With the theory of social consciousness from Part 2 as the foundation of sociology, the text discusses how various societies are formed and change both statically and dynamically. The result envisions the development of individual freedom and equality, ultimately culminating in the establishment of a global communal society.

Based on this theoretical framework, the practical issue of 'ethnicity' emerged as a challenging problem in Japan's situation from the end of the Taisho era to the early Showa period (1920–1930). For Takata, this presented an opportunity to test sociology's analytical capabilities in practice.

The Origin of Takata's Ethnological Studies

The origins of Takata's focus on ethnicity can be traced back to the Taisho period. Takata recalled how the concept of ethnicity suddenly emerged in his mind during his return home in 1919 (Taisho 8):

> *When I wrote 'Principles of Sociology,' nothing occupied my mind more than class. For me, dominated by cosmopolitan tendencies, ethnicity held very little significance. However, later, the great fact of ethnicity arose from the depths of my mind [...]. I must have cried out internally, wondering what to do with this fact of ethnicity [...]. I realized that while considering the future of class, we must also consider the future of ethnicity. I also thought that certain measures addressing class issues would often bring new difficulties to ethnic issues.*
> (Takata, 1934, p. 19)

The essential framework of Takata's ethnic theory first appeared in 'A Personal View on the Race Problem' (Takata, 1919), published in the Osaka's newspaper *The Mainichi* . Beginning with the lament that '*our country's proposal for racial equality principles was ultimately buried in ambiguity,*' this article is crucial for understanding Takata's ethnic theory. As indicated in its opening, Takata's conception of ethnic theory addressed the issue of racial discrimination and inequality between nations during World War I. In other words, at the root of Takata's ethnic theory lay dissatisfaction with racial discrimination, particularly in America and Australia.

In America, the Gentlemen's Agreement of 1908 (later developing into the Immigration Act of 1924) and in Australia, the Immigration Restriction Act of 1901 implementing the White Australia Policy (relaxed for people of color in 1956 and abolished in 1973) were enacted. Japan's government objected to these trends and proposed ethnic equality clauses to the League of Nations, but these were ultimately not included. This is what was meant by 'buried in ambiguity.'

How is racial and ethnic discrimination created? Takata identified three factors: '(1) Contempt arising from differences in cultural levels, (2) Aversion arising from differences in cultural content, (3) Aversion due to ugliness in physical characteristics such as appearance and hair.' He argued that racial discrimination was fundamentally about 'cultural antipathy or aesthetic aversion,' with commonly cited economic causes being merely secondary (Takata, 1920, pp. 185–188).

However, these were general observations. The real issue confronting Takata was how to respond to the actual disregard for racial equality principles. Specifically, how to eliminate discrimination against Japanese people and people of color.

Would this require military or economic power comparable to the imperial powers? Takata firmly rejected this idea, arguing it would only lead to Japan's isolation. Nor did he believe in revising unequal treaties and laws, as discrimination was rooted in the national sentiment of discriminating countries rather than in state policies. He argued that measures to eliminate discrimination through state power or international conventions would ultimately fail. Thus, Takata concluded that only 'cultural elevation' of the discriminated ethnic groups could eliminate discrimination against different ethnic groups (Takata, 1920, p. 188).

What did he mean by 'cultural elevation'? In modern terms, it means the cultivation of mass culture—opening up culture, previously monopolized by experts, to the general public. 'It means liberating social classes that are almost completely disconnected from culture from their constraints and allowing them to participate in the enjoyment and creation of spiritual culture' (Takata, 1920, 193). He particularly advocated increasing cultural opportunities for workers and women.

What, then, would become of nations and ethnic groups that had already achieved 'cultural elevation,' or conversely, those that neither could nor would achieve it? Takata continued with his predictions.

Primitive and weak races would be suppressed and eventually eliminated by superior races of advanced civilized nations. However, these superior races would also suffer from declining birth rates and eventually weaken. *'Thus, might not only races with moderate culture remain on Earth?'* (Takata, 1920, p. 194). This was one of Takata's predictions. But he had another, particularly emphasizing inter-ethnic exchange: *'The development of transportation has shortened the distance between continental ends to that of small islands [...]. The mixing of races will continue for millions of years [...]. Blood mixing will occur thoroughly, and humanity will become a single race as it was in primitive times'* (Takata, 1920, p. 197).

Thus, Takata concluded this article by stating, *'How could one distort scholarship to flatter the yellow race? Future population changes in each country will surely prove the above propositions'* (Takata, 1920, p. 199). While these were indeed still predictions rather than academically refined thoughts, there is no doubt that 'A Personal View on the Race Problem' was one of the ideas that would later develop into theories of state and class, then ethnic theory, and ultimately a theory of world society. This is what we aim to clarify below.

An Overview of Takata's Sociology

When organizing Takata Yasuma's sociology, it's useful to consider several key concepts. There is the 'Third Historical View,' which posits that population growth creates division of labor and differentiation, which in turn determines social change. The concept of 'association' was devised to examine this in detail. While considering the scope of this 'association' as a society, he distinctly separated it into 'partial society' and 'total society.' Takata's sociology is characterized by his systematic use of these concepts to analyze all forms of society. Furthermore, his uniqueness lies in not positioning the family as the smallest unit of 'association' nor finding nations or ethnic groups at the final stage of 'association.' Rather, his concept of 'association' ultimately extended to all of humanity. This distinctive social perspective of Takata's emerged quite early, as evidenced in the following quote:

As social density increases and people come into contact with a wider range of others, they move away from narrow concepts like specific families or nations, and develop thoughts about the human world, directing their attention to this broader view. Cosmopolitanism, which considers humanity and the world, eventually questions the dignity of specific states and classes, leading to individualism that thoroughly respects the individual. (Takata, 1923, p. 319)

This passage appears in 'Changes in Class Foundations' included in *Thoughts on Class* (1923), and records show it was written in 1911 (Meiji 44).

Human associations create society. Societies naturally vary in size. The largest ultimate form is world society as a 'total society.' No matter how large a society is, as long as other societies can be posited outside it, it remains merely a 'partial society.' This is the fundamental thought of Takata's sociology.

This sociological thought progresses from *Society and State* (1922) through *Theory of Ethnicity* (1942) to *Theory of World Society* (1947). The Table 6.1 below shows this genealogy.

In the next section, following this table, we will review the overall picture of Takata's sociology as it represented the 1930s.

Table 6.1 The total picture of Takata's sociology

	1919–1924	*1925*	*1926–1934*	*1935–1946*	*1947–*
General Sociology	*The Principles of Sociology*	*Introduction to Sociology*	*A Study of Social Relations*	*Outline of Sociology*	
Specialized Sociology	*The Division of Labor*	*On Class*	*Class and the Third Historical Perspective; The State and Class*	*The Theory of Power*	
Synthesized Sociology	*Personal Views on the Race Problem; Society and the State*			*The Theory of East Asian Peoples*The Theory of Ethnicity*	*The Theory of World Society*

Based on Takata (1957, p. 144), created by the author. * indicates additions by the authors

'TOTAL SOCIETY' IN *SOCIETY AND STATE*

What is society? Broadly speaking, it is 'association,' and narrowly speaking, it is 'consciousness of unity.' What kinds of societies exist? Examples include religious organizations, political parties, classes, professional organizations, industrial unions, ethnic groups, families, local organizations, and states. Among these, Takata calls those that are neither self-sufficient nor closed 'partial societies.' Being neither self-sufficient nor closed means they can be grouped under higher-level concepts. Thus, 'total society' was positioned as that which integrates 'partial societies.' 'Total society' means 'on one hand, the accumulation of all associations maintaining close mutual connections' and on the other hand, it signifies a 'relational element' that 'relates' to 'the people participating in these associations' (Takata, 1922, pp. 12–13).

With this as a premise, 'world society' is identified as the ultimate and largest 'total society.' 'As communication between various parts of the world becomes frequent, if we seek a range that encompasses all social associations, there exists only the world society or the society as the humanity.' However, 'total society' does not necessarily mean world society. 'Total society' can be either large (world society) or small (closed ethnic groups or states) as long as it is a self-sufficient group. Above all, 'the range of total society is the range of a self-sufficient and closed organizational network of associations' (Takata, 1922, pp. 15–17).

There are three types of 'association' in 'total society.' The first is the unified will of all members, the second is the unified will of some members, and the third is various 'fibrous associations' between members. Takata likens these somewhat difficult-to-understand modes of 'association' to reinforcing steel, bricks, and cement. That is, first, the unified will forms the skeleton of 'total society' like reinforcing steel, the partial unified will is like the bricks laid upon it, and the third 'fibrous association' is like the cement poured into the gaps (Takata, 1922, pp. 77–79).

When tracking this network of associations—that is, the range of communication—through the flow of history, one notices its tendency to overcome regional and spatial barriers. 'The so-called spatial tension capacity of association (die räumliche Spannungskapazität einer Vergesellschaftung) is already attempting to become global beyond the national scope. Unified solidarity mostly establishes its foundation where this network of individual associations is woven. The complication of partial associations and their internationalization should be recognized as an expression of the regional liberation of these individual associations.'

Moreover, Takata elaborates on this spread of communication networks that breaks ties with geographical connections: 'The de-territorialization of total society can mean two things. One is that the scope of partial societies becomes unrestricted by territory, and the other is that the most comprehensive total society is not limited to the scope of one state or region but increasingly becomes global' (1922, pp. 274–275). Here, Takata reads 'the tendency of total society to deviate from the scope of the state.'

However, it must be noted that this was discussed only as an abstract possibility and did not reach the point of depicting actual instances. At the stage of writing *Society and State* in 1922 (Taisho 11), there were no concrete examples that could illustrate 'total society' with specificity. It did not go beyond Takata's imagination. 'Total society' needed realistic entities like East Asian peoples or world states to become concrete.

'TOTAL SOCIETY' IN *THEORY OF ETHNICITY*

There were two main points made in the previously discussed 'A Personal View on the Race Problem.' One was that ethnic groups or nations with moderate cultural levels would survive. This theory was further developed in Chapter 9, 'The Circulation of Ethnic Groups,' of his 'Theory of Ethnicity.' The other point was that increased interaction between multiple ethnic groups would lead to fusion into larger ethnic groups, which was thoroughly discussed in Chapter 10, 'Theory of Ethnic Fusion.' Thus, what remained mere predictions in 'A Personal View on the Race Problem' underwent scholarly examination in 'Theory of Ethnicity.' Moreover, he expressed his lament that 'although the past one or two centuries are said to have significantly reduced class gaps within nations, one could say that the relationship between these colored races and white people has not improved' (Takata, 1942, p. 52). This echoes his lament from 'A Personal View on the Race Problem' from over 20 years earlier. The aim of Takata's ethnic theory was to explore the true nature of racial and ethnic discrimination that showed no signs of improvement.

What, then, was ethnicity for Takata? 'Ethnicity is not total society itself. It goes without saying that various partial groups are included within total society, but they are not included within ethnicity. Ethnicity is ultimately just a partial society, merely one that carries particularly important significance among partial societies and extends across an extremely broad range of life' (Takata, 1942, p. 28).

If ethnicity is a 'partial society,' conflict with another 'partial society' that does not share the same values is unavoidable. If conflict could be avoided, it would be through the existence of something that transcends ethnic frameworks and parochial consciousness. Indeed, ethnicity, like class, is a 'partial society' with strong associational consciousness. However, there are elements that can drive wedges into this association.

Thus, Takata answers the question, *'What factors or circumstances will form a unified world culture?'.* Science, technology, and economics are cited as elements that transcend the narrow-minded consciousness of ethnicity, class, or 'partial society.' 'Among all cultural contents, there are parts that most easily shed ethnic and class characteristics. These are the domains governed by purposive rationality, namely the domains of science, technology, and by extension, economics.' The movement to break down parochialism using these as wedges becomes 'societalization of interests,' 'rationalization,' or 'purposive rationality.' First, through 'imitation and assimilation accompanying increased communication density and population mobility,' and then through the increased importance of purposive rationality, culture moves toward unification. In other words, 'the worldliness of culture is the loss of its ethnicity, and this loss should be seen as primarily dependent on the function of intellect' (Takata, 1942, pp. 94–95).

However, at this point, Takata's description takes a turn. He suggests that leaping directly from ethnic parochialism to 'total society' would still go against rationalization. To reach world society, one must overcome the barriers of states and ethnicities. But there are stages to this process. Identifying these stages is important, and Takata finds this in what he calls 'broad ethnicity.' The concrete ideal is 'ethnic harmony.' 'Going against this [societalization of interests] trend and maintaining a policy of national isolation will lead to the weakening and eventual decline of the ethnicity itself.' However, *'hastening the path of societalization of interests, forgetting sacrifices for ethnicity, and loosening ethnic control'* leads to self-destruction. Takata believed that 'ethnic harmony' was necessary to avoid this (Takata, 1942, p. 225).

There was a time when 'ethnic harmony' could be spoken of as an ideal. How did Takata understand 'ethnic harmony'? First, it meant *'creating solidarity of destiny through the state, making them realize they do not have separate destinies, and bringing about contact in all aspects of life.'* Second, it meant *'protecting what appears to be the legitimate interests of ethnicities and sheltering their lives'* (Takata, 1942, pp. 224–225). This assertion might be an ideal insofar as it presupposes movement toward human society and world society through 'broad ethnicism.'

As for 'how the formation of a global ethnicity is possible,' it occurs through the 'mixing of blood' (Takata, 1942, pp. 202–210). Takata imagines two paths toward achieving blood mixing. The first is the activation of ethnic exchange. However, while blood mixing progresses through the development of transportation, this remains a distant future. Therefore, as a realistic path, the following process can be considered, which is the second path. As culture develops, ethnicities undergo member differentiation, gradually weakening internal ethnic bonds. However, bonds don't just keep weakening. As old bonds weaken, new bonds form with similar members outside the ethnicity. In other words, *'while internal cohesion weakens, external cohesion is increasingly prepared. As this process progresses, barriers between ethnicities are gradually removed, and historical progress moves toward forming an ethnicity encompassing all ethnicities'* (Takata, 1942, pp. 211).

The goal is the 'association' of 'total society.' 'The association of total society includes ethnic association as an important part while being formed through the intersection of many other associations, and therefore sometimes includes even group associations that move in directions opposite to ethnic association, that is, associations that try to oppose it, as one of its parts' (1942, p. 28). However, since it aims for 'association' with 'opposing groups,' traditional 'nationalism' becomes problematic. Thus, 'broad ethnicism' was devised.

> *Past centuries were an era of narrow nationalism. Only through this were ethnic unification and the formation of nation-states completed. And at that time, such broad ethnicism had not yet emerged. When there was a need to think beyond the state, abstract humanity or world was immediately considered. However, with the progress of capitalism, sociological circumstances, that is, circumstances governing association and separation, completely changed. In other words, adhering strictly to nationalism in the narrow sense and relying solely on it is the way to destroy ethnicity.* (1942, pp. 143–144)

In short, *'broad ethnicism'* is nothing other than *'that which is established through this opening up, as the shortening of distances accompanying the progress of material civilization makes everything large-scale and thus forces ethnicities to open up one corner of their closure.'* Thus, it was declared that *'nationalism without the backing of broad ethnicism is now merely a relic of the past'* (1942, p. 144).

As shown above, what flowed consistently from *Society and State* through 'Theory of Ethnicity' to 'Theory of World Society' was the concept of 'total society' as a 'self-sufficient and closed organization of association networks' (Takata, 1922, p. 17). This represents the scholarly refinement of young Takata's dream of human society (the humanity) as a society, a cosmopolitan world. And what pushed forward the writing of 'Theory of World Society' was none other than the global movements after World War II. The construction of a world state was no longer a dream with the United Nations, created by learning from the lessons of the League of Nations. 'Total society,' which previously only appeared in incomplete forms such as states or 'broad ethnicity,' finally revealed its complete form through the establishment of world society.

However, one more point must be added here. Like the establishment of 'broad ethnicity,' the fact is that the establishment of world society is achieved not through science and technology itself but through the advancement of 'weapons and tactics.'

'Just as forced organization intervenes in the structure of total society within the scope of a single country, force also intervenes in the structure of global total society.' In other words, *'in international relations, at least under the rule of democratic principles, and therefore in modern times, equality between states and between ethnicities has become a principle, but in fact, differences in overall power including economics and culture naturally lead to the establishment and intervention of forced relationships.'* The 'forced relationships' mentioned here refer to former conquest states, modern imperialism, or colonies, that is, economic, political, and cultural subordinate relationships (Takata, 1947, pp. 72–73).

Certainly, the negative aspects of 'force intervention' are strong. However, Takata reframes this positively. The results of subordinate relationships are *'first, close contact and unity between both parties'* and *'second, the intersection of interests between both parties.' 'In short, the function of force in world society fundamentally lies in the artificial formation of basic society. While forming direct associational, whole-personal, indefinite-purpose associations that would not form spontaneously and corresponding organizations through force, it attempts to transform and purify these into spontaneous associations, that is, internal associations, through internal cultural and blood assimilation, adaptation, and changes in ideas. [...] Although the harm and disasters of war and other international conflicts themselves are appalling, this socializing effect within spheres of influence itself seems undeniable'* (Takata, 1947, pp. 73–75).

As we have seen, this line of argument can be traced back at least to 'Theory of Ethnicity.' What's interesting is that this was stated immediately after the defeat in the war. Even after becoming the occupied rather than the occupier, he continued to consistently make such assertions. *'The dramatic progress in weapons and tactics now makes us consider the formation of a world state an urgent matter, while fundamentally shaking the traditional view that sees this as merely conceptual. Until the recent past, a world state was treated as a fantasy or idealist's dream. At present, it could be said to be an approaching trend'* (1947, p. 48). This was written in 'Theory of World Society' in the third year of occupation. While one might be tempted to read this as a jab at the occupying forces, that would be mistaken. Such an interpretation would be as off-target as concluding that 'Theory of Ethnicity' and 'Theory of East Asian Peoples' were justifications for 'Japanese imperialism's' occupation policies. Here, Takata is speaking about the irony that 'the dream held by sociologists at the beginning of the 20th century,' namely the cosmopolitan dream of humanity becoming one, would be brought about as a result of war. Looking at history, military force has been at least one effective factor in world integration. Takata merely repeated this point.

From Total Society to World Society

The aim of this chapter was to situate Takata Yasuma's vision of 'total society' within his lifelong sociological endeavors. It primarily represents the progress of Japanese sociology from the 1920s through the 1940s (from the Taisho era through the early Showa period), centering on the 1930s. As we have seen in this chapter, Takata's singular trajectory— beginning with 'A Personal View on the Race Problem,' proceeding through *Society and State* and *Theory of Ethnicity*, and finally reaching the post-war *Theory of World Society*—could be traced with 'total society' as its axis. 'Total society' was an isolated, self-sufficient, and closed society, and as long as these conditions were met, its scale was not an issue. Rather, it was an eminently analytical concept that could be applied to understanding ethnicities, nations, and, ultimately, world society. It represented Japanese sociology's attempt in the 1930s to conceptualize the world.

REFERENCES

Takata, Y. (1919). *Shakaigaku Genri [Principles of Sociology]*. Iwanami Shoten. (In Japanese).

Takata, Y. (1920). *Gendai Shakai No Shokenkyu [Studies in Contemporary Society]*. Iwanami Shoten. (In Japanese).

Takata, Y. (1922). *Shakai To Kokka [Society and State]*. Iwanami Shoten. (In Japanese).

Takata, Y. (1923). *Kaikyu Ko [Thoughts on Class]*. Juekaku. (In Japanese).

Takata, Y. (1934). *Hinsha Hissho [The Poor Shall Triumph]*. Chikura Shobo. (In Japanese).

Takata, Y. (1942). *Minzoku-ron [Theory of Ethnicity]*. Iwanami Shoten. (In Japanese).

Takata, Y. (1947). *Sekaishakai-ron [Theory of World Society]*. Chugai Shuppan. (In Japanese).

Takata, Y. (1957). *Gakumon Henro [Academic Pilgrimage]*. Toyo Keizai Shinposha. (In Japanese).

CHAPTER 7

The Development of Empirical Sociology (Social Research) from the Pacific War to the Post-war Period: Focusing on Teizo Toda

Abstract From the 1910s, poverty studies were being conducted in Japan among economists, social policy researchers, and Marxist scholars. Under their influence, there were growing calls for social research in sociology, which had previously been overly theoretical. In this context, Teizo Toda was the first to systematically present empirical sociology in Japan. Beginning with historical research on families, he later studied various research methods, including statistics, monographs, and questionnaires, publishing a groundbreaking work titled *Social Research* in 1933.

As a sociologist during the transition period from armchair sociology to empirical, positivist sociology, he was more conscious than later generations about the relationship between general sociology, theoretical sociology, and social research. He clarified the interdependent relationship between social research and sociology. In terms of research, he was fortunate to have access to statistical data from Japan's first national population census conducted in 1920. In an era without computers, Toda used individual census forms to advance his empirical family research.

Furthermore, Toda organized academic activities in Japanese sociology and made significant contributions to its institutionalization. Through his management of the 'Japan Sociological Society' and leadership of the University of Tokyo's Faculty of Letters' Sociology Research Department,

S. Mitupova, K. Yoshino, *Sociology in Japan*, Sociology Transformed, https://doi.org/10.1007/978-3-031-91347-1_7

he nurtured many talented individuals and researchers. After the war, he also collaborated in public opinion surveys.

Keywords Theory of social research • Empirical sociology • Sociology of family • National population census • Chicago school • Quantitative research • Statistical survey method

EMPIRICAL SOCIOLOGY

When was empirical sociology or social research introduced in Japan? Social research studies have existed in Japan since the 1910s (early Taisho period). Takano Iwasaburo (1871–1949) from a statistical perspective, Yamazaki Kakujiro (1868–1945) from a social policy perspective, and Yamaguchi Tadashi (1887–1943) from a social work perspective each conducted their respective research to address poverty and labor issues. However, serious theoretical and methodological research in social research emerged with Toda Teizo (1887–1955), who is the focus of this chapter. If Takada Yasuma laid the foundation for theoretical sociology, then Toda can be said to have established the foundation for empirical sociology, particularly centered on family sociology. His work can be divided into four major areas: first, family sociology; second, research on private property, occupation, and social status; third, population and community studies; and fourth, social research theory.

Toda graduated from the Philosophy Department (Sociology Major) of Tokyo Imperial University's Faculty of Letters in 1912 (Meiji 45). His graduation thesis focused on the development of Japan's family system. From 1920 to 1922, he studied in the United States. After returning to Japan, he took a position at Tokyo Imperial University. At the university, he taught courses including 'Research on Poverty Relief,' 'Social Research Methods,' 'Introduction to Sociology,' and 'Family.' It is particularly noteworthy in modern Japanese sociology history that courses related to social research were established at Tokyo Imperial University in the 1920s. Meanwhile, Toda also contributed to the institutionalization of sociology. While supporting the 'Japanese Institute of Sociology' founded by Takebe and Yoneda, he was also involved in the establishment (May 1924) and management of the newly formed 'Japan Sociological Society.'

If we were to narrow down Toda's academic contributions to two points, they would be as follows: First, he introduced social research methods as an empirical approach, contributing to the advancement of sociology and social sciences. Second, he studied the family as an organization beyond just a collection of individuals, empirically analyzing its structure and functions.

The Development of Social Research Theory in Japan

Toda published his Tokyo Imperial University graduation thesis, titled 'Research on the Development of the Family System in Japan,' in the *Annual Report of the Japanese Institute of Sociology* (First Year, Combined Issues 1 & 2, December 1913). This was a study of the historical transitions in family systems throughout Japanese history. Meanwhile, he published 'On Life Survey Methods' (*Kyuhin Kenkyu* Vol. 7 No. 6, June 1919) as a paper dealing with methodology for researching contemporary rather than historical families. The content of this brief paper was as follows:

Social research aims to record human living conditions as they are. This is necessary for two reasons: first, to improve society, and second, for academic research. In other words, social research is conducted for both social policy needs and scientific purposes. Of course, these are not separate entities. Toda's fundamental position was that without academic research, it would be impossible to address the social issues that emerge daily.

Specific social research methods included 'statistical methods,' 'monographs' ('individual survey methods'), and 'questionnaire survey methods.' While each had its unique characteristics, Toda perceived them as having flaws. According to Toda, 'statistical methods' lacked depth and could vary depending on the researcher's handling. He further stated that statistics inevitably become inaccurate because they attempt to express qualitative matters quantitatively. While this seems contrary to current evaluations of statistics, such views were commonly found in Japanese sociology during the introduction of statistical methods.

'Monographs' (individual survey methods) had the advantage of being able to examine individuals' lives in detail but had the disadvantage of being time-consuming. Furthermore, monographs represented only a small portion when viewed within the whole, and from the researcher's standpoint, there was the drawback of difficulty in finding suitable subjects.

Regarding 'questionnaire methods,' Toda pointed out flaws while considering surveys by specialized investigators like those in British parliamentary survey reports. He noted that investigations by survey committees were formulated in people's minds, and it was unclear whether they reflected actual facts.

As social research was a new methodology not yet familiar in Japanese sociology, Toda, in the 1910s, seemed to view none of these methods as entirely satisfactory. Particularly regarding statistical surveys and question-naires, he held prejudices similar to those of theory-oriented sociologists of the time. However, an opportunity for a complete reversal in this evalu-ation would come with his study in America.

What Toda Learned in America

What Toda learned from American sociology was not theory but social research techniques. His study experience at the University of Chicago in the 1920s brought about a major transformation in his perspective. The University of Chicago, during Toda's study period from 1920 to 1921, was approaching its golden age in social research (Faris, 1967).

As Toda stated, 'While in Chicago, there were lectures by people like Albion W. Small (1854–1926), Robert E. Park (1864–1944), Ernest W. Burgess (1886–1966), and Ellsworth Faris (1874–1953). Small and Park's lectures were just as written in their books. Faris's lectures were very interesting. In America, they spared no expense in conducting sur-veys for social work. As a result, social research studies were advancing.'

Apart from the Chicago School, Toda was influenced during this period by F. Stuart Chapin (1888–1974) and Mary Ellen Richmond (1861–1928). Chapin published *Field Work and Social Research* the same year Toda arrived in Chicago. Chapin was a student of Giddings at Columbia University and was then a professor of economics and sociology at Smith College. In 1922, he moved to the University of Minnesota and served as president of the American Sociological Society. He developed social research theory utilizing statistical, quantitative, and experimental meth-ods. Chapin's famous 'Three Types of Field Work' classification—(1) case-work, (2) sampling, (3) complete enumeration—was later adopted in Toda's *Social Research*.

The other person who influenced Toda was Mary Ellen Richmond. She was a practitioner, leader, and theorist of American charitable activities. Her main work was *Social Diagnosis* (1917). Richmond advocated the necessity of investigation, diagnosis, and treatment for problem-solving with charitable activity clients. The important thing was collecting the cli-ent's Social Evidence, which came in three types: (1) real evidence, (2) testimonial evidence, and (3) circumstantial evidence. The importance of interviews with subjects and testimonies from family and acquaintances was also emphasized in Toda's *Social Research*, along with Richmond's name.

These two individuals did not have particularly close ties with Chicago School sociology. Moreover, the Chicago School is known for developing ethnographic qualitative research studies. However, as M. Bulmer points out, two research methods have traditionally coexisted in Chicago sociology: 'field study or social survey' (life history method, personal documents, case studies, participant observation) and 'quantitative research method.' While the Chicago School is immediately associated with qualitative research development, this view is not entirely accurate. Quantitative research in Chicago sociology, though a 'neglected tradition,' definitely existed in the 1920s (Bulmer, 1981). Toda correctly grasped this trend. As a result, in *Social Research* published after his return, he gave equal weight to both qualitative individual survey methods like life history and case studies, and quantitative research methods. While he had been negative about it before his study abroad, what Toda absorbed with fresh excitement during his American studies, centered in Chicago, was rather the quantitative method.

Social Research (1933)

As mentioned, *Social Research* was Japan's first work in this field. Let's briefly examine its contents. According to Toda, social research is a method to understand the facts of social life as accurately as possible. He explains the necessity of social research thus: 'Life is action and practice.' While 'decisions' determine practice, decisions alone are insufficient. One must correctly understand reality, identify effective means for practice, and select appropriate methods. Toda believed that social research provides the basis and evidence for making these selections appropriately. Social research can be utilized both for academic purposes in university settings and for practical applications in society. It can scientifically clarify the basis and conditions of human behavior while also presenting materials for policies that guide people toward appropriate actions.

With this basic understanding, the table of contents of *Social Research* lists the following topics:

Table of Contents:

Chapter 4: Partial Survey or Selection Survey Methods
Chapter 5: Individual Survey Methods or Case Study Methods
Chapter 6: Survey Preparation
Chapter 7: Survey Organization

In Chapter 1, Toda explains social research in terms of 'narrow' and 'broad' definitions. Social Survey or Social Research was initially used by those pursuing social improvement work. The narrow definition refers to surveys for social work aimed at solving immediate issues and contributing to social improvement. In contrast, the broad definition involves surveys of people's social lives from a wider perspective. While his earlier paper 'On Life Survey Methods' distinguished between 'need for social improvement' and 'need for academic research,' the latter corresponds to the broad definition of social research.

Chapter 2 discusses the relationship between sociology as a scientific discipline and empirical sociology or social research. Sociology is fundamentally a science organized on the basis of empirical facts about social life. Therefore, social research is essential for gathering empirical social facts. Conversely, organizing empirical sociology requires pre-prepared conceptual tools that theoretical sociology provides. Toda explains this using F. Tönnies's three-part structure of sociology: theoretical/pure sociology, applied sociology, and empirical sociology or social geography.

Chapters 3–5 detail specific methodologies: complete/statistical surveys (including census and demographic surveys), sampling methods (classified into typological, application, extraction, and connection methods), and individual survey methods (detailed observations of individual units, referencing the Chicago School's life history method and works by Richmond, Thomas, Znaniecki, and Shaw).

The final chapters (6 and 7) provide supplementary material on preparatory and organizational work necessary for practical social research implementation.

THE SIGNIFICANCE OF TODA'S SOCIAL RESEARCH THEORY

The significance of Toda's social research can be articulated in several key aspects. First, he positioned scientific sociology and empirical sociology/social research as mutually dependent entities. Within the historical context of modern Japanese sociology's development, it is particularly noteworthy that he strongly emphasized the importance of empirical sociology and social research, aiming to establish sociology as 'a science organized fundamentally on empirical facts about social life' rather than letting it remain merely academic sociology or imported knowledge.

Second, he appropriately grasped the relationship between theoretical construction, hypothesis formation, and social research. He recognized that empirical sociology 'is established only through 'numerous individual studies' provided by social research,' and that organizing empirical sociology requires reliance on 'pre-prepared conceptual tools,' with 'theoretical or pure sociology taking on the task of providing such conceptual preparation.'

Third, he introduced the distinction between 'narrow' and 'broad' social research. The distinction between 'broad' social research referring to 'general surveys of people's social lives' and 'narrow' social research 'directly serving social improvement work' was particularly decisive in Toda's survey theory development and is notable in the history of modern Japanese social research and observation.

Fourth, he attempted detailed methodological considerations of 'complete survey or statistical survey methods,' 'partial survey or selection survey methods' (sampling), and 'individual survey or case study methods.' Moreover, in light of the development of 'broad' scientific social research, we can observe his tendency to emphasize 'complete survey' (statistical survey methods) and 'partial survey' (sampling) methods.

This systematic approach helped establish the foundation for modern social research methodology in Japan, bridging theoretical and empirical approaches while maintaining both academic rigor and practical applicability.

Toda Teizo's Family Research and Survey Methods

In Toda Teizo's sociological research, his most significant achievements were in the field of family sociology. Previously, family research had primarily focused on institutional studies. In contrast, Toda studied the family as a social group, as this approach had rarely been taken before. He believed that empirically studying the composition and function of family group life was most important in sociology. These findings were compiled in *Family Research* (1926), and particularly *Family Composition* (1937) is evaluated as a significant work in this field.

In *Family Composition* (1937), considered Toda's masterwork, through the process of preceding family research works such as 'Family Research' and 'Family and Marriage,' he addressed three areas of study that had been embryonic and intermingled in his early papers: (1) research on family systems, (2) research on the relationship between family functions and external social functions, and (3) research on the group nature of families. However, in this book, the focus was specifically limited to exploring (3) in terms of 'the compositional forms of families in contemporary Japan.' The table of contents was structured as follows:

The book began with a preface and introduction, followed by Chapter 1 on 'The Group Characteristics of Family' and Chapter 2 on 'Japanese Family Composition.' In the introduction, based on the fundamental idea that 'the family as a small group is based on people's internal demands, which take socially acceptable forms under direct control of conditions imposed by external society,' Toda developed his famous definition that 'family is a personal fusion based on the affection between spouses, parents and children, and their close relatives, and is a dependent and communal relationship founded on such emotional fusion.'

Chapter 2, 'Japanese Family Composition,' was devoted to empirical analysis and verification of the theoretical hypothesis that 'family is a small group based on emotional fusion of a small number of closely related people.' The survey data used for this empirical verification was primarily statistical material from the first national population census of 1920. Using a 1/1000 sample of the total 55,963,053 people and 11,210,000 households nationwide, Toda conducted detailed statistical analyses distinguishing between those in pure kinship relationships and others in each household.

Through this extensive statistical analysis, Toda quantitatively revealed several facts about Japanese family composition at the time: (1) increase in nonfamily living persons (about 10.3% of the total population), (2) reduction in family size (national average of 4.5 members), (3) changes in 'patriarchal families' due to the development of modern industrial institutions, family members working outside, development of transportation, and decrease in family businesses, and (4) the predominance of relatively simple two-generation families, with traditional multigenerational families comprising less than 30% of all families.

CHARACTERISTICS OF TODA'S FAMILY RESEARCH

Several distinctive features characterize Toda's family research. First is his definition of family. Beginning with an examination of various theories, Toda defined family as 'a personal fusion based on the affection between spouses, parents and children, and their close relatives, and a dependent and communal relationship founded on such emotional fusion.' Rather than viewing family from an institutional perspective, he developed a small family bond theory from the viewpoint of social groups, social processes, and social relationships, stating that 'the family as a small group is fundamentally based on people's internal demands, which take socially acceptable forms under direct control of conditions imposed by external society.'

Second is Toda's elucidation of the group characteristics of Japanese families. He consistently analyzed the structural characteristics of groups. He conceptually distinguished between 'family forms respected by the people' ('traditional family composition') and 'families as they actually exist' ('current family composition'), attempting empirical clarification using census statistics. He identified empirical statistical trends such as the characteristics of patriarchal families centered on parent–child bonds in Japan ('continuity of family lineage' and 'emphasis on family line preservation'), a gradual decrease in patriarchal families, a shift toward nuclear families, an increase in nonfamily living persons ('increase in people unable to find internal stability within families'), and simplification of family member types.

Third is his method of empirical analysis. Among the three survey methods used in *Social Research* (statistical survey method, selection survey method, case study method), Toda primarily adopted statistical analysis using census data through sampling methods. The hand count from 1/1000 sampling copies must have required tremendous labor and effort. Since this research began after the Cabinet Statistics Bureau's *Overview of First Census Results Using Sampling Methods* (1924) was published, it took over a decade until its completion and publication in *Family Composition*.

Toda began with a theoretical hypothesis based on the small family bond theory that 'family is a small group based on emotional fusion of a small number of closely related people' and 'is a dependent and communal relationship founded on such emotional fusion.' His empirical analysis method was to verify this hypothesis—a hypothesis-verification type of survey analysis. Questions remain about whether census statistical data could adequately verify Toda's theoretical hypothesis. Could such statistical data measure people's internal demands, mental attitudes, and emotional fusion within family groups? Could it truly measure dependent and communal relationships? Even as hypothesis-verification empirical analysis, one might question whether the theoretical explanation of family group characteristics in Chapter 1 and the empirical analysis of Japanese family composition in Chapter 2 were sufficiently corresponded. These questions about Toda's work remain to be addressed (Toda, 1933).

THEORETICAL VERIFICATION AND METHODOLOGICAL LIMITATIONS

In the 1930s, Toda developed a social research theory in Japanese sociology. It was groundbreaking that empirical sociological research was conducted in his specialized field of family studies. However, his inclination toward statistical and quantitative methods following his return from studying in America may have resulted in the relative neglect of other forms of social research. Research in areas such as ethnographic monographic studies, historical sociological research, folkloric surveys, and qualitative research had to be carried out by other scholars.

The chapter on 'Sociology and Social Research' that appeared in *Social Research* was removed in the post-war revised edition, *Shakai Chosaho* (*Methods of Social Research*). Toda's perspective was that the relationship between sociology and social research formed a circular structure: sociological theories create concepts and directions for social research, and survey results, in turn, generate new theories. However, in Toda's case, he ultimately remained focused on the first half of this process—verifying theory. We must note that he did not develop the latter half: building new hypotheses from field research.

REFERENCES

Bulmer, M. (1981). Quantification and Chicago Social Science in the 1920s: A Neglected Tradition. *Journal of the History of the Behavioral Sciences, 17*, 312–331.

Faris, R. E. L. (1967). *Chicago Sociology 1920–1932*. The University of Chicago Press.

Richmond, M. E. (1917). *Social Diagnosis*. University of California Libraries.

Toda, T. (1933). *Shakai Chosa [Social Research]*. Jityosya. (In Japanese).

CHAPTER 8

The Birth of Rural Sociology in Japan: The Contributions of Suzuki Eitaro

Abstract Eitaro Suzuki (1894–1966) was the first to establish systematic rural sociology in Japan. He entered Tokyo Imperial University and studied state theory under Togo Takebe. However, due to differences with Takebe, he transferred to Kyoto Imperial University for graduate studies, where he studied under Shotaro Yoneda. In 1925, he obtained his first position at Gifu Higher School of Agriculture and Forestry (now Gifu University). Having translated works on state theory by Spencer and Hobson, his interest lay in theoretical methods of analyzing the state. However, he was also interested in whether these analytical methods could be applied to actual real-world problems. Encouraged by the principal of Gifu Higher School of Agriculture and Forestry to research rural communities, he also studied American rural sociology literature. In this way, Suzuki narrowed his focus to Japanese rural society as a practical subject for testing his methodology. Then in 1940, he published his monumental work *Principles of Japanese Rural Sociology* (Suzuki, *Nihon Noson Shakaigaku Genri [Principles of Japanese Rural Sociology]*, Jichosha, 1940).

Keywords Natural village (shizen-son) • Village spirit (mura-no-seishin) • Rural sociology (noson-shakaigaku) • Ie System (ie-seido) • Social districts (shakai-chiku) • Cumulative community • Social consciousness (shakai-ishiki) • Stem family (chokkei-kazoku)

S. Mitupova, K. Yoshino, *Sociology in Japan*, Sociology Transformed, https://doi.org/10.1007/978-3-031-91347-1_8

AMERICAN RURAL SOCIOLOGY

In the mid-1920s, when Suzuki began his research on Japanese rural society, empirical research in Japanese sociology was virtually nonexistent. Suzuki himself was immersed in studying social science methodology, far removed from rural research. However, the 1920s American rural sociology was at one of its peaks in its developmental history. Charles Josiah Galpin (1864–1947), Newell LeRoy Sims (1878–1965), Dwight Sanderson (1878–1944), and other theories influenced Suzuki. He particularly valued the theories of Pitirim A. Sorokin (1889–1968) and Carle Clark Zimmerman (1897–1983). What he learned from these studies was primarily the methodology for sociological research of rural areas. Facing the entirely new research field of Japanese rural sociology and needing to deal with concrete problems, it was extremely beneficial for Suzuki to follow the empirical paths pioneered by foreign scholars. However, while learning theory is relatively easy, applying it to Japanese society requires considerable effort. While consistently aiming to apply it to Japanese rural areas, he critically absorbed Western theories.

Where did Suzuki place his emphasis? It was on determining the fundamental regional society in Japanese rural areas and how to define it as a sociological concept. The idea that 'determining the concrete regional form of the fundamental society in rural areas' should be the first important task that emerged early on.

This definition of fundamental regional society would later be organized into the concept of a natural village. He critically absorbed Galpin's concept of Rurban Community and Sorokin's concept of Cumulative Community (Sorokin et al., 1930). However, this was more of a creative application rather than a simple one. Specifically, Suzuki early on aimed to determine Japanese village society as a community in concrete regional terms and attempted to capture it as a unified entity above the Cumulative Community.

How did Suzuki's own empirical research on Japanese villages progress? Detailed surveys were conducted on all eight villages in Sakahogi Village, located in the eastern part of Gifu City. Using this as his field, he investigated the administrative villages and old villages (natural villages) existing within the city.

Of course, all the work Suzuki faced was new ground. He had to realize step by step his policy of determining the fundamental regional society of Japanese rural areas, conducting sociological analysis of the social structure there, and theoretically and empirically confirming its unity as a community. This had to be executed from the new academic standpoint of sociology. While there was much research on Japanese rural areas, none took this new stance. While theoretical precedents could be found abroad, Suzuki's goal was ultimately to establish Japanese rural sociology. He had to work alone to seek data from a new perspective on Japanese village life, confirm its meaning, and build it into theory. He had to explore various aspects of life and select necessary, valuable data from them. Needless to say, this work required extensive knowledge, originality, and unwavering effort.

JAPANESE RURAL RESEARCH IN THE EARLY SHOWA PERIOD

Around 1930, a trend toward empirical research of rural social life began to emerge. Needless to say, agriculture, rural villages, and farmers held greater importance in Japanese national life then than they do today. Interest in rural social life was growing in agricultural economics and agricultural policy studies, with notable research results emerging from their respective perspectives. In particular, Kunio Yanagita and his disciples were enriching their knowledge from the standpoint of folklore studies. One can immediately see in *Principles of Japanese Rural Sociology* that Suzuki used these various scientific findings as valuable source material. However, Suzuki needed to collect, analyze, and interpret facts from his own standpoint. He published this methodology in 1932 as Nouson Shakai Chosaho (Methods of Rural Social Research).

At that time, surveys of rural social life were becoming active in fields such as agricultural economics, agricultural policy, economic history, human geography, local education, and folklore studies due to the so-called empirical trend. While various survey procedures and item proposals were emerging, Suzuki's stood out for being sociological and systematic. Explaining his survey methodology, Suzuki stated, 'This survey focuses primarily on clearly revealing the relatively independent form of regional society ... That is, by determining the spatially expressible domains of various societies, it divides the domain of human relationships that form relatively independent groups on the territory, and clarifies rational survey areas necessary for subsequent more detailed and partial surveys' and 'It observes and copies facts from all aspects of life in such regional societies at roughly the same depth.'

Principles of Japanese Rural Sociology aimed to regionally determine the fundamental society in rural areas, observe the entire domain of social life conducted there in terms of regional expansion, and capture it as a unified structure.

Principles of Japanese Rural Sociology is not merely research about Japanese rural areas but also a study of rural sociology methodology. This is why Suzuki frequently conducted surveys and collected data on Japanese rural social life. Going beyond a mere collection of Japanese rural facts, he aimed to ultimately establish Japanese rural sociology. In Chapter 1 of *Principles of Japanese Rural Sociology*, he stated that 'Japanese rural sociology must have methods and domains that adequately conform to the reality of Japanese rural areas,' noting that the basic structure of Japanese rural society clearly differed from that of other countries. However, since Suzuki's academic foundation was in sociology, his theoretical logic and concepts relied on sociology.

Suzuki's position was that while Japanese rural sociology might have specific limitations regarding its research domain, the main methodological issues concerned the research domain, and there was no difference from general sociology regarding the constructive principles of the laws and concepts handled therein.

Principles of Japanese Rural Sociology (Suzuki, 1940)

Principles of Japanese Rural Sociology is a major work that attempted to systematically interpret the overall structure of rural villages. Among its theoretical contributions, we must note its determination of the basic social unit of Japanese rural villages and its concrete regional and theoretical analysis of this unit—the so-called natural village theory. Additionally, it provided a sharp analysis of the sociological understanding of Japanese rural families, making valuable contributions to Japanese family sociology. Suzuki frequently argued that the basic units of socialization in Japanese rural society were the village and the family and that the theoretical elucidation of these two elements formed the main cornerstone for establishing Japanese rural sociology. The table of contents of *Principles of Japanese Rural Sociology* lists the following themes:

Table of Contents of *Principles of Japanese Rural Sociology*

Chapter 1: Japanese Rural Sociology

Chapter 2: Research Methods in Japanese Rural Society
Chapter 3: Social Structure of Japanese Rural Areas
Chapter 4: Family and Family-Centered System in Rural Areas
Chapter 5: Social Groups in Japanese Rural Areas
Chapter 6: Social Relations in Japanese Rural Areas
Chapter 7: Unity of Natural Villages and Their Social Consciousness
Chapter 8: Spheres of Common Interest
Chapter 9: Social Differentiation of Natural Villages
Chapter 10: Classification of Japanese Villages

To briefly introduce the content: Chapters 1 and 2 develop the theory and methodology of Japanese rural sociology. Chapter 3 presents preliminary conclusions about the structure of basic regional society in Japanese rural areas. Detailed explanations leading to these conclusions are discussed in Chapters 5–8. Among these, Chapter 7, 'Unity of Natural Villages and Their Social Consciousness,' contains Suzuki's original assertions and forms the core of the book. Chapter 5, 'Social Groups in Japanese Rural Areas,' classifies various groups recognized in Japanese rural areas from the perspective of village society as a Cumulative Community, examining how these groups accumulate within the regional sphere centered on the village or extend beyond it. In this process, Suzuki distinguished between primary, secondary, and tertiary social districts to determine the basic regional society of Japanese rural areas.

Here, Suzuki established three categories: social groups, social relations, and social spheres distributed and accumulated in these districts. Furthermore, he presented individual interactions as social processes, treating these as fundamental relationships, and used them as analytical concepts for rural social structure. As we will see later, this is also applied to family analysis in Chapter 4, 'Family and Family-Centered System in Rural Areas.' Suzuki's rural family theory, as mentioned earlier, is not only one of the main cornerstones of his Japanese rural sociology but also contains numerous important arguments for Japanese family sociology.

After developing the static structural theory of Japanese rural areas, Chapter 9 deals with dynamic development. This was an extremely difficult chapter for Suzuki and remains somewhat experimental. Chapter 10 is positioned as an appendix describing the actual classification of Japanese villages.

JAPANESE VILLAGES AND FAMILIES

Determining the basic regional social unit of Japanese rural areas is the primary prerequisite for sociological consideration. This must be done both theoretically and empirically. Suzuki learned much from American rural sociology for this purpose, particularly referencing the Rurban Community theory and its developments from the 1920s to the 1930s. However, the history of farm management and settlement establishment in America is shallow. Moreover, American farm households undergo more dramatic transformations compared to Japan, with a stronger corporate management nature. In America, not only are Community forms diverse, but they present extremely fluid and complex aspects, including the movement or multiplication of Community Centers, absorption into cities, accompanying changes in Community boundaries, and the rise and fall of Neighborhoods within Communities. By the 1930s, these phenomena could no longer be adequately explained by the Rurban Community theory.

In contrast, Japan had village life with a long tradition of settlement. Long before the establishment of Japanese capitalism, there were villages with high stability both as geographical settlements and social life units. The history of resident and family settlement was also long. This is what Suzuki focused on. His task was to theoretically elucidate, from a sociological perspective, how families functioned as the basic social units constituting Japanese rural society.

Suzuki used three categories—social groups, interpersonal social relations, and spheres of common interest—to analyze rural social life, dividing them into primary, secondary, and tertiary social districts based on their regional distribution and accumulation. He famously demonstrated that these accumulations were most dense in the secondary social district, showing that rural communal society could be established there. This secondary social district often corresponded to former villages (natural villages) that existed before the implementation of the municipal system. However, Suzuki sought to prove that such districts existed as socially unified entities with independent self-sufficiency and autonomy. While the accumulation of groups, social relations, and social spheres was an important condition for such unity, proving their existence as self-sufficient, autonomous unified societies required more. Suzuki found this in the effect of common social consciousness that existed at the foundation of such accumulation, which village members shared and which guided and regulated their behavior. He applied the term 'natural village' to the social unity realized in the secondary social district, seeking the range of self-sufficient, autonomous effects that appeared and operated in the accumulation of groups, social relations, and social spheres and in the common social consciousness, various village norms, customs, and institutions.

From this perspective, Suzuki's concept of natural village is not merely following Sorokin's theory of Cumulative Community society. Nor does it seek the basis of community in the establishment of coordination born from functional complexes of accumulating institutions, agencies, and services, as in Galpin's Rurban Community theory. What establishes the natural village is the normative social life principle that autonomously drives the village, existing at the foundation of the cumulative whole. This unifying effect of this principle can be summed up as the 'village spirit.'

VILLAGE SPIRIT

This normative life principle lives within villagers' daily lives and serves as their behavioral standard. How is it established and maintained? Suzuki expresses this as residing in the web of individual social processes among villagers. It can be read in the village's customs, practices, and institutions. The spread of this web is also the spread of the village's common social consciousness. Using this web as a foundation, groups were organized and accumulated by accepting the village spirit. Japanese villages have long existed within such social boundaries. For example, in Edo period villages, the unifying effect of village communal consciousness was maintained through strict regional administrative boundaries, economic self-sufficiency, and high social and cultural closure. Naturally, understanding rural society with such traditions has its unique characteristics. Suzuki's distinctive natural village theory is established by empirically confirming the secondary social district based on former villages and finding the root of its social unity in the effect of normative social life principles rooted in village life traditions.

'What is a village? Sociologically speaking, it is the self-sufficient, unified effect of social consciousness conducted by residents within a defined area through their shared individualistic social consciousness content.' Suzuki states that this definition 'merely speaks of one cross-section of the temporal flow of historically developing villages, and the full picture of villages flowing through time should be called a history of spirit or historical development of a set of meaning systems' (Suzuki, 1940, p. 445).

Thus, the village spirit constantly adheres to and controls the direction of village social processes. Various institutions and customs within the cooperative body exist based on spiritual approval. Concrete expressions of village spirit can be seen in such institutions and customs.

SOCIAL RELATIONS

Besides classifying social groups, Suzuki also classified social relations (Suzuki, 1940, Ch.6). Social relations are what Suzuki also terms social process types. These are social bonds between individuals, and their content and continuation often depend on individual subjective judgment. Moreover, Suzuki believes that alongside social processes, they often form the village's latent structure at the foundation of the cooperative body and are subject to regulation by the village spirit. As an empirical description, he lists concrete forms of social relations, particularly important ones such as lending and borrowing, gift-giving, assistance, cooperation, and other practices, and meeting forms (their relatively fixed forms, including village gatherings, communal work, communal dining, rituals, funerals, weddings) as important elements, stating that these indicate the village's social boundaries and have regulatory power as expressions of village norms and behavioral principles.

In essence, Suzuki attempts to show whether the fundamental conditions that make it a socially unified entity are present at the foundation of the Cumulative Community of the secondary social district. This is nothing other than the self-sufficient unity of social consciousness effects.

SUZUKI'S FAMILY THEORY

As mentioned earlier, Suzuki considered the family a basic unit of socialization. His family theory has made important contributions to Japanese family sociology. While Suzuki's family theory primarily focuses on sociologically explaining the Japanese 'ie' (household), since 'ie' is also a historical form of family, it's crucial to understand how his theory explains family in general.

Suzuki distinguishes between 'ie' and family as follows: 'The unified existence of Japanese family life is called the family cooperative body or simply "ie," and when observing the personal relationships of family members constituting it, it is appropriate to call it family.' 'The term family is appropriate when considering the family group with particular focus on its

group nature. This term is most appropriate when discussing modern Western urban nuclear families, as they are nothing more than groups. In my thinking, which recognizes the essence of "ie" as a social phenomenon in our country beyond its group nature, there is a need to consider "ie" and family separately' (Suzuki, 1940, pp. 139, 143).

'Today, almost all rural families in our country are what we call stem families, and they also constitute "ie".' While this description broadly indicates the key points distinguishing between 'ie' and family, we must understand this in more detail.

The mutual relationships between family members, or the institutions that integrate the family, become the foundation for the existence of 'ie.' In other words, '"ie" is an institution and need not be a group' (Suzuki, 1940, p. 244). Moreover, as family emphasizes its group nature, its normativity and integration are lost, while conversely, as 'ie' emphasizes integration and institutional nature, its group nature weakens.

What Is 'Ie'?

Suzuki considers Western urban conjugal families to directly demonstrate this essence. He views the various characteristics of family bonds that Toda Teizo cites as incidental elements arising during the continuation of sexual relationships, and while acknowledging that these characteristics exist, he considers it a separate issue of whether they are indispensable qualities of family. Thus, interest in the basis of the integration of nuclear family bonds, as described by Toda, becomes minimal. While these urban families have orders regulating life, according to Suzuki, these are based on the general principles of humanism, utility, and instinct, not ethics aimed at family life itself, but rather ethics regulating relationships between individual family members. In other words, they are nothing more than what Suzuki calls 'groups' (Suzuki, 1940, pp. 140, 178).

In contrast, since the essence of 'ie' is sought outside its group nature, its institutional aspect is emphasized, establishing a distinction from family. According to Suzuki, while 'ie' often constitutes a family, this is not a requirement for being 'ie,' or indispensable for its existence. While family exists as individual family members connected horizontally through interpersonal social relationships, 'ie' exists connected vertically through time and generations. 'What makes "ie" what it is is that it is rather a temporal flow connected to past history and future development.' 'While family is a horizontal relationship of existing individuals, "ie" is rather a relationship

between generations, and strictly speaking, "ie" is a spirit' (Suzuki, 1940, p. 148).

'Ie' is a spirit. This spirit can be recognized in the unified activities of current family members and is embodied in the relationship connecting such unified activities with those in the past and future. 'If one insists on calling it group activity, it is not only a relationship among existing individuals but also a relationship with past ancestors and future unknown descendants,' says Suzuki. This spirit is at the center of 'ie.' The household head is its embodiment and symbol. Members of 'ie' first connect to this center and thereby establish mutual relationships. 'Ie' is established through this spiritual unity (Suzuki, 1940, p. 148).

A Constellation of 'Ie' Member

Suzuki explains the constellation of 'ie' members as follows: While conjugal families are little more than the sum of relationships between individual members, in patriarchal families (including stem families), members first unite with the center to connect with each other. The center is the spirit of 'ie,' symbolized in personal form by the household head. Members of 'ie' are arranged in a specific constellation according to their social distance from the household head. Relationships between constellations are not free interpersonal relationships but relationships in terms of constellation formality, thus relationships in terms of connection to the center. Therefore, this constellation should be called the constellation of 'ie' itself. This is the ordering of the web of individual bonds at the foundation of 'ie.' The spirit of 'ie' permeates this, forming the basis of 'ie's' unity and wholeness.

However, conjugal families lack such a constellation. Here, members relate directly to each other. Yet even in any individualistic, liberal conjugal family, there are certain disciplines in being a husband or child. However, these are principles governing general human relationships, primarily principles of humanity, utility, and instinct. While conjugal families also have certain behavioral norms between spouses and children, and, in that sense, have their own constellations, the ethics between spouses are those of male–female relationships and love, and ethics with children are general ethics of age hierarchy, strong and weak, educator and educated. These are not ethics aimed at family life itself. While such families have unity, it

comes from the effect of instinctual principles between men and women, parents and children, or from legal guarantees.

These are social life principles between individuals, with individual happiness in its most legitimate sense as the ultimate indicator. This contrasts with 'ie's' social life principle, which subordinates individual life to the goal of maintaining and developing the 'ie.' While Suzuki thus defines the nature of conjugal family bonds, he does not evaluate the existence of normativity and institutionality seen in such family life. This seems related to Suzuki's essential definition of family bonds in general, as mentioned earlier. Suzuki's interpretation of spousal and parent–child relationships as basic relationships in nuclear families, his interpretation of the lack of ethics aimed at family life itself, and his interpretation of the basis of unity that exists nonetheless likely differ considerably from the modern nuclear family theory's approach to family bonds. Regardless, Suzuki's family theory develops on this juxtaposition of 'ie' and family.

ANALYSIS OF THE 'IE' SYSTEM AND FAMILISM

While we have discussed the juxtaposition of 'ie' and family as a fundamental characteristic of Suzuki's family theory, it goes without saying that *Principles of Japanese Rural Sociology* primarily focuses on investigating 'ie.' Suzuki presents unique and sharp analyses from various angles about the normativity and institutional nature of 'ie,' the unifying effect of the 'ie' spirit, and various aspects of 'ie' life.

Additionally, Suzuki offers an original perspective in discussing familism. He states that 'as long as family is recognized as an institution in any ethnic society, there exists familism at least to that extent.' He defines familism as the attitude of recognizing, protecting, and fostering the family that a society acknowledges as an institution—for example, in the case of Japanese 'ie,' this includes ancestor worship, beliefs and practices, and customary institutions that make 'ie' the unit of social life. His discussion of the relationship between family ('ie') and society and the significance of familism permeating the web of social relations among members within the family ('ie') is particularly innovative.

REFERENCES

Sorokin, P. A., Zimmerman, C. C., & Galpin, C. J. (1930). *A Systematic Source Book in Rural-Urban Sociology* (Vol. 1). University of Minnesota Press.

Suzuki, E. (1940). *Nihon Noson Shakaigaku Genri [Principles of Japanese Rural Sociology]*. Jichosha. (In Japanese).

CHAPTER 9

Basic Trends in Post-war Japanese Sociology and Marxism

Abstract Japanese sociology faced its major turning point after the Pacific War. The GHQ (General Headquarters, the Supreme Commander for the Allied Powers) occupation policies included both the purge of public officials and educational system reforms. Scholars who held professorships at major universities or key positions in government research institutions and were deemed to have cooperated with the war effort were removed from their positions. Sociologists like Yasuma Takata and Masamichi Shinmei were among those purged. The removal from public office was not lifted until after the signing of the San Francisco Peace Treaty in 1951, which ended the occupation. During this period, sociologists who had been active before the war fell silent.

Meanwhile, those who were students during the war years were part of a generation that suffered direct material and psychological damage. They developed a sense of having been 'deceived' by the pre-war generation. This erupted as resentment and criticism from the younger generation of sociologists toward their seniors. Their primary objective became reforming Japan's conservative, oppressive, and patriarchal institutions and rebuilding Japan as a new 'democratic' nation. The researchers tackling these issues were themselves required to be conscious of the need to be democratic individuals.

This fundamental characteristic has defined post-war Japanese sociology. This chapter will outline the directional changes in sociology from the post-war period to the present day.

S. Mitupova, K. Yoshino, *Sociology in Japan*, Sociology Transformed, https://doi.org/10.1007/978-3-031-91347-1_9

Keywords Post-war sociology (Sengo Shakaigaku) • Japanese national sociology • Rural sociology (Noson Shakaigaku) • Mass society theory (Taishū shakai ron) • Structural-functionalism (Kozo-kino shugi) • Educational reform (Gakusei Kaikaku) • Marxist sociology (Marukusu shugi shakaigaku) • Consumer society (Shohi shakai) • American sociology

JAPANESE NATIONALIST SOCIOLOGY

The aftermath of World War II brought about a profound transformation in Japan, leading to the collapse of Japanese imperialism and the subsequent establishment of American occupation. This significant shift in power dynamics raised critical questions for Japanese sociology, particularly regarding its role in addressing the moral implications of war responsibility. On the one hand, sociologists grappled with the pressing need to confront the implications of Japan's militaristic past, while on the other, they faced the challenge of determining the future trajectory of Japanese society and how sociology could contribute to this evolution. Despite the urgency of these issues, the exploration of war responsibility within the field of sociology has been notably inadequate. Prominent figures such as Eikichi Seki[1] and Hiromichi Kawai[2] had previously advocated for a concept of 'Japanese Sociology,' which framed sociology as a form of nationalism and a supportive science for the state. However, this perspective was largely rejected, leading to the dismantling of traditional sociology that had previously served as the ideological backbone of the absolutist monarchy. The rejection of pre-war sociological frameworks, particularly from a positivist standpoint, resulted in a superficial examination of the history of Japanese sociology. This oversight hindered a comprehensive understanding of how to reconstruct sociology in the post-war era, particularly in terms of establishing a discipline that genuinely serves the needs and aspirations of the populace. As Japan sought to redefine its identity and societal structures in the wake of defeat, the challenge remained to develop a sociology that not only acknowledged past failures but also actively contributed to the rebuilding of a more equitable and just society.

Around 1935, the concept of 'Japanese Sociology' emerged from an exclusionary perspective, seeking to explain the significant stagnation of the discipline by asserting that it had failed to align with the social realities of Japan. This viewpoint proclaimed the inherent superiority of the

Japanese people's fundamental spirit and equated the imperial ideology of 'Hakko Ichiu'[3] with the principles of sociology. In contrast, positivist sociology, championed by scholars like Teizo Toda, emphasized the necessity of empirical and demonstrative research. This approach also acknowledged Japan's social realities and challenged the unscientific methodologies of 'Japanese Sociology,' leading to noteworthy advancements in the field. However, this positivist approach ultimately became intertwined with the imperial state, promoting the 'expansion of the household spirit' under the guise of 'family sociology.' It advocated for the establishment of 'a new order in East Asia' and the notion of 'world harmony.' Similarly, under the label of 'occupational sociology,' it encouraged the idea of 'service in one's profession' and called for a 'transformation of occupational views,' ultimately compromising its scientific integrity in the face of imperial authority, thus converging with the tenets of 'Japanese Sociology.' As a foundational step toward reconstructing sociology in the post-war context, there was a renewed emphasis on the importance of 'empirical research of reality.' It was asserted that 'the primary task of our sociology is to conduct a concrete and realistic analysis of Japanese society' (Fukutake, 1948, p. 246). This assertion reflected a necessary acknowledgment of the role empirical research had played prior to the war, although this critical point was largely overlooked. Previously, Ikutaro Shimizu had vehemently opposed the notion that 'the strong demand to seek research subjects in Japan inevitably leads to an adherence to Japanese methods in research.' In the post-war period, however, Shimizu shifted his stance, declaring that 'the central focus of sociology must always be on real issues.' He emphasized that 'methodological problems would reach a certain stability through the experience and accumulation of research' (Shimizu, 1948, p. 321), thereby underscoring the need for unrestricted empirical research on social realities. This evolution in thought marked a significant turning point in the development of sociology in Japan, as it sought to align itself more closely with the pressing issues facing society.

Reflecting on the state of sociology prior to the war raised the fundamental question, 'What is sociology?' and prompted a reevaluation of the relationship between 'Marxism and Sociology.' Around 1935, Fukutake noted that sociology had failed to offer effective guidance for reconstructing society after the past framework was dismantled by defeat, warning that neglecting this issue could lead to sociology being overshadowed by official Marxism. This crisis awareness transformed positivist sociology into a proponent of sociological reconstruction, emphasizing 'value-neutrality' in science and the integration of 'theory and research.' Consequently, the focus shifted from 'What is sociology?' to 'What is society?' with an emphasis on clarifying social reality. Shimizu pointed out that the relevance of sociology as an independent science is less important than understanding that all facts and issues arising in social life fall within its scope (Shimizu, 1948, p. 321).

When sociology is described as 'the science that examines human social communal life' (Fukutake, 1948, p. 13), its subject matter is seen as a natural outcome of the positivist approach. The individuals studied in sociology are not just abstract entities; they are real, tangible human beings, and sociology centers on their 'communal life.' However, the in-depth examination of real societies is not solely the domain of sociology. What distinguishes sociology is its focus on social reality as the direct subject of inquiry in its phenomenological aspect. In this context, while discussing specific individuals, the conversation shifts to the abstract interactions and communal lives of these individuals, often ignoring class relations. The movement from phenomenon to essence is rejected; instead, by analyzing phenomena, the inherent contradictions within society are revealed, while methods that consider reality from a class standpoint are generally dismissed.

POST-WAR REFORMS AND SOCIOLOGY

From the 1950s to the 1960s, mainstream Japanese sociology focused on rural sociology, family sociology, and theoretical history research. In a sense, this was an extension of pre-war Japanese sociology. Japanese sociology, which had developed as an imported discipline, began with introducing the latest theories. The sociology of Takebe, Yoneda, and Takata exemplifies this approach.

However, global sociology gradually shifted toward social research methods. Japanese sociology followed suit, turning toward empirical research focusing on families and rural communities. While post-war Japanese sociology maintained these pre-war themes, its content took an entirely different direction.

One of the post-war reforms was land reform. Large landholdings were prohibited, and land was sold cheaply to tenant farmers. This transformed agricultural management and farming households' lives, shifting from large-scale to small-scale farming. In response, post-war rural sociology studied the changing lives of families engaged in small-scale farming.

The prominent Japanese sociology journal *Shakaigaku Hyoron* (*Japanese Sociological Review*) dedicated its 1950 inaugural issue to 'The Pre-modern Nature of Japanese Society.' Japanese landlords, along with zaibatsu conglomerates, symbolized Japan's 'pre-modernity' and 'feudalism.' The post-war Japanese agenda, promoted by GHQ and supported by the Japanese government, was to overcome pre-modernity and thoroughly democratize society. Family and village structures retained 'pre-modern feudal vestiges' (Nihon Jinbun Kagakuyokai, 1951). Sociology needed to contribute to overcoming these elements, which supported the popularity of rural and family sociology. Research fields expanded beyond farming villages to fishing villages.

Particularly notable research achievements in Japanese sociology during the late 1950s came from those who hadn't published before the war or those newly educated in sociology after the war. The watershed moment between pre-war and post-war periods emerged around 1957–1958, symbolized by the publication of 'Lecture Series in Sociology' (9 volumes, 1957–1958) edited by Tadashi Fukutake, Rokuro Hidaka, and Toru Takahashi, and the *Dictionary of Sociology* (1958). These works were primarily written by the wartime and post-war generations and showed energetic absorption of American sociology by young researchers.

Theoretical sociological research continued to accumulate. While the pre-war focus was mainly on German and French theories, interest rapidly shifted to American sociology after the war, largely due to the Allied occupation and limited information from defeated Germany. By the late 1950s, Structural-Functionalism by Talcott Parsons and Robert K. Merton, and survey methodology by Paul Lazarsfeld were actively introduced and examined.

THEORY OF SOCIAL SYSTEM

The demand for 'theoretical sociology' expressed in this manner created an opportunity for the introduction of Parsons and others' social system theory and action theory, leading to the emergence of theorists like Kenichi Tominaga. It goes without saying that this 'theory' stood in direct opposition to Marxism. The perspective of structural-functional analysis perceives the whole within the interdependence of its various elements and captures their interrelationships; however, it does not understand these relationships in terms of contradiction and conflict, nor does it grasp them dialectically as the unity of opposites. Furthermore, in this context, materialism is denied and both matter and ideas are analytically decomposed into various elements and variables. The criteria for the selection of these variables are considered pragmatic, relating to the understanding of empirical problems.

In the social system theory, the relationship between two individuals is taken as the simplest element, where the interaction between self and others stabilizes through the establishment of complementary expectations. This complementarity is said to be made possible by a common value orientation. From this, norms arise and become internalized within the personality. The institutionalized norms lead to the distribution of roles, resulting in a hierarchy of positions within the system based on those roles. As a result, the class theory found in Marxism is replaced by a theory of social stratification. In other words, the theory of role behavior interprets the class issue as a matter of occupational roles within the industrial social system. It views class domination, derived from the ownership and non-ownership of production means, as relating to the distribution of social resources such as tools and rewards.

This theory, by framing the problem of social order as one of norms and role distribution, denies the conflicts and contradictions between classes, rationalizes the existing bourgeois order as a natural order, and blinds itself to the social development from capitalism to socialism. It goes without saying that this is a critical standpoint that must be reiterated.

A position advocated by Akira Takahashi, Kotaro Kido, and Joji Watanuki aimed to address the deficiencies in historical and comprehensive perspectives found in American sociology and social psychology through a 'critical incorporation' of Marxism. These scholars sought to re-evaluate topics such as mass society, small groups, and organizations—subjects often discussed in American sociology without historical context—by integrating Marxist concepts like class, system, and monopoly capital. Their paper, 'Mechanization of Groups and Organizations,' published in *Modern Thought* in 1957 within the issue titled 'The Machine Age,' exemplifies this approach. In this work, mass society is analyzed through the dual structural principles of 'organization' and 'atomization,' suggesting that 'the structure of mass society is modeled as a combination of impersonal organizations like machines and impersonal, atomized individuals.' The authors characterize the masses as individuals homogenized by 'the logic of the system,' where 'immediate classes are condensed into an internal existence of the system as the masses, before becoming oppositional classes' (Takahashi et al., 1957, pp. 110, 113).

From this, 'the confrontation between "class" as the logic of revolution and "masses" as the logic of the system' allows 'mass society' to be conceptualized, while the 'mass society' itself, which 'embodies' both the logic of revolution and the logic of the system, is thus defined in a transhistorical and morphological manner. In other words, what lies behind the theory of 'mass society' is a transcendental, ideological schema of individuals, groups, and society, wherein the Marxist concepts of class, system, and revolution are employed merely as tools to embellish the ideological framework with conventional everyday terminology.

Rokuro Hidaka[4] argued that cooperation between Marxism and non-Marxism is necessary not only at political and social levels but also ideologically and academically. He stated that 'the two different systematic thoughts or academic frameworks should creatively incorporate each other's methods or theories into their own systems,' and that this would have 'a positive significance' (Hidaka, 1960, p. 172) However, some scholars point out that it is impossible to introduce 'methods' and 'theories'—the crucial structural materials that make a specific theory a 'system'—into one's own framework without falling into conciliatorism or eclecticism. In the case of Marxism, what is learned from other academic fields consists of research achievements grounded in concrete facts, which cannot constitute essential methods or theories within that academic system.

In the case of sociology, according to Hidaka, the 'unfortunate antagonism between sociology and Marxism' is caused by political reasons external to academia. He states that the criticism from the Marxist side, which comprehensively denies sociology as a 'bourgeois reactionary science,' is nothing more than ideological dogmatism. When criticism against sociology is made from the Marxist perspective, it is said to critique a subjective and metaphysical (= anti-dialectical) method or thought common to various forms of sociology, which can be as numerous as the sociologists themselves. It goes without saying that evaluations of individual sociologists' research must be considered based on their specific facts. The theory of 'peaceful coexistence' between Marxism and sociology was expressed without acknowledging the ideological character and class nature of sociology. At the same time, this conciliatory position is established by equating Marxism with revisionism.

For example, Hidaka argues that 'we should distinguish between the academic evaluation of Bukharin's achievements and Bukharin's political downfall as a politician.' He evaluates Bukharin for being 'well-versed' in the accomplishments of individual bourgeois sociology and for 'creatively accepting' its 'results,' but he posits that the Marxist sociology that Bukharin developed by systematizing the 'results' of bourgeois sociology is based on equilibrium theory, and is thus unrelated to Marxism. Similarly, those whom Hidaka views as having 'creatively developed' Marxism—such as Henri Lefebvre and Fei Xiaotong—were also individuals who, captivated by the positive aspects of certain sociologists and the 'results' in specific fields, sought to incorporate the subjective methods of sociology into Marxism, eventually drifting away from Marxism.

Hidaka criticizes the phenomenon in which Japanese Marxism has become 'rigid, misapprehending reality, and clinging to dogmatism.' To overcome 'the most dangerous dogmatism, arterial sclerosis,' he advocated for the active incorporation of other thoughts within one's own framework. From this standpoint, Hidaka countered the claims of Yoshio Shiga in the October 1959 issue of *Zenei* regarding 'Contemporary Revisionism in Japan' as sectarianism and dogmatism. His critique contained valid points regarding the then-current Japanese Marxism; however, he failed to understand that Marxism is not developed through the introduction of different methods and thoughts or through mutual exchanges with non-Marxism but is enriched and creatively developed through practical engagement grounded in a transformative perspective of current realities. This lack of understanding reflects a limitation in the understanding of Marxism from the conciliatory standpoint held by Hidaka and others (Hidaka, 1960).

Tanaka tackled this difficult issue and played a certain role in the ideological struggle. Tanaka viewed the attitude of thematically denying the issue of 'primary groups' due to the ideological character of bourgeois sociology as leftist opportunism while also opposing rightist opportunism that involves 'unprincipled methodological compromise and abandonment of ideological struggle' (Hidaka & Kitagawa, 1958). He regarded 'primary groups' as spontaneous phenomena and argued that Marxism must engage with the analysis from a practical standpoint, not through the theoretical understanding of primary groups themselves but by analyzing class relations, addressing international conditions where the term 'primary groups' is never mentioned, and explaining capitalist production relations. Here, the issue of 'primary groups' is approached not as a subject of 'group theory' but as a problem of spontaneous consciousness and ideology and is practically framed as an issue of organization and leadership within class struggle.

Marxist sociology, studied before the war but suppressed during wartime, regained momentum under the post-war theme of Japanese modernization and abolishing feudalism. Its influence became particularly prominent after the 1959–1960 Anpo protests. The *Contemporary Sociology Series* (6 volumes, 1963–1964) featured nearly half its authors declaring Marxist positions.

Sociology for 'Democratization'

The reconstruction of Japanese society after the Asia-Pacific War centered on 'democratization'[5] and the establishment of a democratic framework, according to sociological perspectives at the time. The focus on democratization reflected a fundamental shift in how scholars and policymakers approached the transformation of Japanese institutions, social structures, and cultural norms in the aftermath of the Asia–Pacific War.

The achievement of this anti-feudal democracy was discussed at that time in two directions: the direction of realizing a free capitalist society in Japan, which aligns with classical bourgeois democracy, and the direction of achieving the People's Democratic Revolution with a vision of a socialist revolution. Within this context, Fukutake advocated for socialist democracy rather than liberal democracy, arguing that any path other than the construction of a socialist society would be reactionary. Of course, the content of Fukutake's notion of 'socialism' was somewhat unclear in terms of class stance, focusing on the nationalization of the means of production and planned economy, which later shifted to the term 'socialization.' Moreover, this idea of socialist democracy was asserted only for a brief period right after the defeat; subsequently, the concept of general 'democratization' was promoted from an Enlightenment perspective, focusing on liberation from feudal families and village communities. This anti-feudal democracy gradually lost its progressive significance during the process of democratic reform initiated by the American occupying forces. The idea of anti-feudal democracy in sociology, under the semi-forced introduction of American sociology, lost its initial closeness to socialism and came to regard American democracy as the ultimate standard. Eventually, 'democratization' was replaced by 'modernization,' taking on an anti-communist role. However, at that time, the ideology aimed at democratizing Japan, even when conflicting with the direction advocated by Marxism, did not possess an anti-Marxist tendency. Instead, there existed a certain loose unity between the progressive aspects of social sciences that advocated for both Marxism and anti-feudal democracy.

Immediately after the war, there was disagreement and confusion regarding the direction Japan should take, even within Marxism. Following the cessation of the February 1 General Strike in 1947, the issue of the struggle against American imperialism was partially recognized; however, it had not yet been positioned as an important strategic goal, and the so-called error of the 'peace revolution theory under occupation' could not be overcome. The criticism of the Cominform in 1950 marked a correction of this error, but the fact that it occurred in the difficult context of the American invasion of Korea, the repression of the Japanese Communist Party, and its illegalization led to the emergence of extreme left adventurism and sectarianism within Marxism. The 1951 program of the Japanese Communist Party was groundbreaking in that it raised the banner of struggle against American imperialism and anti-imperialist struggle, but on the other hand, it overestimated the continuation of the semi-feudal parasitic landlord system and failed to correctly position aspects such as the transformation of the absolutist emperor system into a traitorous bourgeois monarchy.

Confusion Among Marxist Scholars

After 1950, the revolutionary direction established by Marxism could be simply stated as the direction of an anti-imperialist and anti-feudal democratic revolution. However, this was tied to a misjudgment regarding land reform and an incorrect analysis of Japan's current situation. Specifically, it mistakenly perceived Japan's dependence on American imperialism as being the same as other colonial subordinate nations. From this arose an adventurous approach that mechanically applied the general tactics of liberation struggles from other colonized countries to Japan, leading to an immediate organization of armed struggle. This also resulted in a subjective and sectarian bias in Marxist theory. There was an overestimation of the emperor system and the parasitic landlord system, along with an underestimation of monopoly capital.

With the onset of the 1950s, the introduction of American sociological theories became pronounced in sociology, and the systematization of sociology using structural-functional analysis methods began to advance. The earlier emphasis on conducting research based primarily on the concrete study of Japan's social realities sometimes led to an easy-going investigative omnipotence and trivialism, which spurred a tendency toward sociological theory.

Shunsuke Osho argued that the motto 'Run toward the facts' must be paired with ongoing reflection on theoretical foundations; otherwise, verification becomes aimless. He promoted an 'operational stance' in sociology as a critique of simplistic survey methods. However, upon closer examination of positivism, it became clear that dialectical materialism was rejected, leading to agnosticism. Osho noted that 'science does not deal with metaphysical hypotheses,' which undermined the connection between 'scientific concepts' and reality, and asserted that the criteria for truth do not align with metaphysical existence. This dismissal of truth as a standard of objectivity ultimately rejected the materialist perspective, viewing the recognition of inherent laws as 'metaphysical' dogmatism (Osho, 1950, pp. 188–194).

Mass society theory also gained popularity alongside structural-functionalism. Originating from J. Ortega y Gasset and K. Mannheim, it became explosively popular in post-war America. Works by D. Riesman, C.W. Mills, and D. Bell became highly popular in Japan. The influential journal *Shiso (Thought)* featured a special issue on 'Mass Society' in November 1956.

ALIENATION IN MASS SOCIETY

Around the same time, Takayoshi Kitagawa described mass society as a collection of homogenized, isolated, and atomized individuals. He analyzed the revival of social solidarity from two perspectives: the ruling class's efforts to enhance integration and the subordinate classes' attempts to form natural groups, especially in workplaces. The concept of 'mass society' was introduced to advocate for the recovery of unity among atomized individuals. This recovery was portrayed as emerging through the formation of 'spontaneous small groups,' including discussions on labor movement activities.

The acceptance of the 'mass society' theory led to a revisionist stance on the theory of 'alienation.' Kitagawa noted that sociology and Marxism split into two paths: one either recognizing sociology or merging it with historical materialism. He claimed that a proposed third path for integrating both would be 'unproductive,' yet the theory of 'alienation' was aligned with this integration effort (Kitagawa, 1963, p. 218).

Here, he highlights the 'increasing sense of alienation' among 'manipu-lated' and 'atomized' individuals as a structural aspect, while the cultural aspect focuses on the conflict between human creations and humanity itself. It critiques the discussion of 'human' alienation in relation to 'scien-tific and technological progress' or 'social differentiation,' arguing that this approach neglects class perspective and is not truly Marxist. The issue of 'nuclear weapons' exemplifies this, as they represent both human achievement and a threat manipulated by a powerful few, trapping the majority in fear. This situation frames the conflict between 'imperialists of the minority' and 'the people of the majority' under the concept of 'humanity,' equating nuclear weapons from both imperialist and socialist countries. Additionally, it posited that the need to understand how the 'logic of the system' (or capital) is linked to public discontent and alien-ation, starting with the problems of 'technology and humanity' and then addressing 'system logic' (Kitagawa, 1963, pp. 4–5).

This perspective is essentially the same as that of the theorists of 'mass society' observed earlier, providing an example of how both conciliatory and revisionist positions can converge at a similar point.

Ikutaro Shimizu introduced Karl Mannheim's concept of 'crab without its shell,' expressing concern about masses of individuals disconnected from their belonging groups. Terms like Riesman's 'other-directed' and Mills's 'cheerful robot' perfectly captured Japanese society's condition from post-war recovery through high economic growth, resonating beyond academic sociology into journalism.

NOTES

1. Seki Eikichi (1900–1939), an advocate of Japanistic sociology, wrote in his article in 1935, 'The great transformation of the world history is now mak-ing it the historical destiny that the Japanese people should become the leader of the world history in place of the European. If this could come true, then the Japanese sociology should become the general and universal sociol-ogy.' Seki envisioned that the Japanese people and Japanese sociology should evolve from a focus on the particular to the universal (Seki, 1943, pp. 325–337).

2. Hiromichi Kawai (1907–1991) insisted, in his Principle of the Japanese Sociology (1943), that the Japanese sociology should bring the 'Japanistic awareness as historical being with particularity and uniqueness' to the Japanese people (Kawai, 1943, p. 143).

3. The Japanese slogan 'Hakko Ichiu' translates to 'all the world under one roof' or 'unify the eight corners of the world.' It was a political slogan that expressed the divine right of the Empire of Japan to unify and expand its influence globally. This slogan became prominent during the Second Sino-Japanese War and World War II, serving as a foundational ideology for Japanese imperialism. It glorified Japan's military aggression and colonization efforts, framing them as a historical mission rooted in the nation's narrative of divine destiny.

4. Hidaka Rokuro (1917–2018) https://apjjf.org/2018/21/mccormack

5. The word 'democratization' appeared as a new and trendy word while the term 'sociology' was no longer considered taboo. In the 1950s, educational reforms mandated the inclusion of sociology courses in general university curricula, particularly for freshmen and sophomores. This led to the establishment of numerous sociology departments and programs within other disciplines, especially at private colleges and universities. A sudden demand for sociologists emerged as American influences permeated various aspects of Japanese society, with sociology being no exception. Among the many American sociological theories that impacted Japanese sociology, the ideas of Talcott Parsons were the most influential.

References

Fukutake, T. (1948). Wagakuni Syakaigaku Saiken no Tameni [For the Reconstruction of Our Sociology]. In *Syakaigaku no Gendaiteki Kadai [Contemporary Issues in Sociology]*. Hyoronsya. (In Japanese).

Hidaka, R. (1960). Shobo Kotonatta Gakumonteki Tachiba no Kyouryoku [Cooperation of Different Academic Positions]. In *Gendai Ideology [Modern Ideology]*. Keiso. (In Japanese).

Hidaka, R., & Kitagawa, T. (1958). *Gendai Shakai Shudanron [Contemporary Theory of Social Groups]*. University of Tokyo Press. (In Japanese).

Kawai, H. (1943). *Nihon Syakaigaku Genri [Principles of Japanese Sociology]*. Shorin-sha. (In Japanese)

Kitagawa, T. (1963). *Sogai no Shakaigaku [The Sociology of Alienation]*. Yuhikaku.

Nihon Jinbun Kagakukai (Ed.). (1951). *Hoken Isei [Feudal Remnants]*. Yuhikaku. (In Japanese).

Osho, S. (1950). Operational Stance and Spatial Analysis of Social Phenomena. *Japanese Sociological Review, 1*, 188–194. (In Japanese).

Seki, E. (1943). *Kokutai to Zentaisyugi [Nationalism and Totalitarianism]*. Seinen Tsusinsha. (In Japanese)

Shimizu, I. (1948). *Shakaigaku Kogi [Lectures on Sociology]*. Hakujitsu Shobo. (In Japanese).

Takahashi, A., Kido, K., & Watanuki, J. (1957). Shudan To Soshiki No Kikkaika [Mechanization of Groups and Organizations]. In *Kikai Jidai [The Machine Age: Modern Thought]*. Iwanami Shoten. (In Japanese).

CHAPTER 10

The Direction of Japanese Sociology: During and After the Cold War

Abstract This chapter explores the trajectory of Japanese sociology from the immediate post-war period through the Cold War era and into recent times. It begins by examining how Marxist sociology evolved in Japan, focusing on debates over its relationship with traditional Marxist thought. The discussion then moves to the 1970s, when mass society theory transformed into new theoretical frameworks including post-industrial society and consumer society theories, followed by the emergence of postmodernist perspectives. The chapter chronicles the institutional growth of sociology in Japanese universities and research centers since the 1950s, documenting its expansion across academic institutions. The analysis concludes by identifying key challenges for contemporary Japanese sociology: developing systematic theories, synthesizing empirical findings, and enhancing international scholarly exchange.

Keywords Japanese sociology • Marxist sociology • Post-industrial society • Sociological education • Academic institutions • International exchange • Postmodernism

Marxist Sociology

The revision of Marxism within sociology has existed as an international trend since the late 1950s in the form of establishing 'Marxist sociology' in the Soviet Union and Eastern European socialist countries. This trend seeks to correct the original intent of unifying the practice and theory of Marxism through 'specific sociological investigations.' In Japan, the possibility of 'Marxist sociology' has also been raised by Seisuke Tanaka. He stated that 'Marxist sociology cannot conclude merely with the establishment of general laws; it must include the process of specific application of those laws and the guidance involved therein' and emphasized that 'sociological research based on historical materialism is integral to the content of scientific socialism and communism.' By doing so, Tanaka related 'Marxist sociology,' which had previously been addressed only in relation to historical materialism, to the theories of scientific socialism and communism (Tanaka, 1965, pp. 90–91).

Tanaka argues that 'Marxist sociology' occupies a space between historical materialism and scientific socialism. However, this does not clarify why it should be labeled 'Marxist sociology' instead of simply 'Marxist social science.' While it's true that the challenges posed by bourgeois sociology go beyond historical materialism, Tanaka's point holds merit. Nonetheless, it is inappropriate to define the specific area of 'Marxist sociology' in advance and determine its connections to the three elements of Marxism—philosophy, historical materialism, or scientific socialism. Attempts to align different branches of Marxism with the divisions found in bourgeois social sciences, like economics, political science, and sociology, often lead to a mechanical separation of these components. This approach underpins the arguments for 'Marxist sociology.' However, it is essential to recognize that these discussions are fundamentally linked to class practice within Marxism. If Marxism is viewed as a dynamic guide for action rather than a rigid doctrine, it must be enriched by the revolutionary practices of the proletariat and their class struggle. Reducing the complexities of strategy and tactics in that struggle to 'Marxist sociology' or 'sociological investigation' is something that true Marxists cannot accept.

Tanaka emphasizes the importance of distinguishing between labor relations, which involve interactions between producers and the material and technical base, and production relations within socioeconomic formations. He argues that while focusing on the material and technical base is a sociological perspective, it is not adequately explained. Tanaka differentiates between the 'technical process' and the 'material and technical base,' asserting that the latter must be understood in relation to specific production relations. He critiques the view that the cooperative nature of labor in large-scale mechanized industries can be seen as a separate labor relation, arguing that this perspective undermines the materialist position on the determinacy of 'material social relations' in Marxism. Tanaka contends that failing to recognize the distinction between production and labor relations leads to an 'economic materialism' that conflates the essence of labor with its phenomenal production relations, ultimately denying the Marxist definition of production relations as independent of human will (Tanaka, 1965, pp. 85–89).

Distinguishing 'labor relations' from production relations and asserting the uniqueness of the former lead, in the case of Tanaka, to a distinction between 'Marxist sociology' and Marxism itself, claiming the uniqueness of the former. Here, we can observe a method that views the issues of technological progress and labor organization as separate from class relationships or, conversely, as defining class relationships. This approach ultimately aligns with the earlier discussed theory of 'alienation.' Regarding the relationship between Marxism and sociology, Takayoshi Kitagawa raises the issue of whether a certain academic field can sufficiently exist under the name of sociology, even while acknowledging the negation of previous sociology (Kitagawa, 1965, p. 15).

Kitagawa discusses the inherent duality of subjectivity and objectivity within sociology, emphasizing that social science must navigate this complexity. He argues for a method that allows for both self-objectification and objectification of the self, suggesting that adopting the perspective of 'developing classes' can harmonize these two aspects. He references Weber's struggle to define social science as a unity of subjectivity and objectivity, particularly in the context of cultural values and historical conflicts. Kitagawa posits that achieving this unity requires a conscious transformation of both the objective and subjective worlds, acknowledging that while the objective reality and the concept of the objective are not the same, the distinction between subjectivity and objectivity is relative. He warns against the pitfalls of idealism that arise when separating the human subject from their practical agency. Furthermore, he critiques the simplistic assumption that subjectivity, as the problem consciousness of the recognizing subject, can easily align with objectivity from a 'class perspective.' In Kitagawa's case, the notion of a 'new true sociology' that seeks to find 'a method that can objectify the self' is discussed in opposition to 'traditional sociology' while standing upon this materialist position. Kitagawa states, 'Following Marx, the inheritance of true sociology and the overcoming of sociology cannot be achieved solely by standing on that position and repeating dogmas; it depends on the application of the permissible methods of its fundamental principles and the efforts and accumulation of internalization of the self.' To prevent the said 'efforts of internalization' from ending up as mere 'critical absorption,' as suggested by mediation theorists, it is necessary to clarify the nature of 'true sociology' (Kitagawa, 1965, pp. 22–32).

THEORIES OF CONSUMER SOCIETY AND POST-INDUSTRIAL SOCIETY

By the 1970s, discussions on mass society, which had been stimulated by the propositions of Marxist sociology, evolved into various forms such as 'post-industrial society theory,' 'consumer society theory,' and 'information society theory.' Works by Jean Baudrillard's *The Consumer Society* (1970) and Daniel Bell's *The Coming of Post-Industrial Society* (1973) became bestsellers in Japan. These discussions collectively formed what would become the postmodernist current. Jean-François Lyotard's 'The Postmodern Condition' (1979), which greatly influenced postmodernist discourse in sociology, stated in its opening that postmodern culture corresponds to 'post-industrial society.'

In postmodernist discourse in Japan from the 1980s onward, the Western model of 'modern civil society' became somewhat relativized. This aspect differed from mass society theory. Generally, mass society theory tended to view mass society as a 'degraded form' of modern civil society and lacked perspective in relativizing modern civil society. This was also true in Japanese mass society theory. While Western societies developed in clear stages (premodern/modern (civil society)/contemporary (mass society)), Japan's situation was more complex as modernization (civil society formation) and mass society formation occurred simultaneously. Apart from some Marxist discussions, there were few perspectives that relativized Western-style modern civil society itself.

From the 1980s to the early 1990s, amid Japan's postmodern trends and bubble economy, there was a tendency to avoid modern seriousness, and practical concerns diminished. However, after the bubble burst and following events like the 1995 Aum Shinrikyo incident and the Great

Hanshin-Awaji Earthquake, the practical and policy-oriented interests of early post-war sociology revived. This coincided with what Masato Hase described as the shift from 'postmodern sociology' to 'sociology of responsibility and justice' (or the 'responsibility and justice-ization' of postmodern discourse) (Hase, 2006). These trends were further strengthened by the 2011 Great East Japan Earthquake and nuclear accident.

THE STRUCTURE OF SOCIOLOGICAL RESEARCH AND EDUCATION

From an educational perspective, the implementation of educational system reforms led to the expansion of higher education. New universities were established one after another, with sociology integrated into their curricula. As a result, sociology experienced such remarkable growth that it was said that 'no other science has shown such striking prosperity' (Usui, 1975, p. 15).

In contemporary Japan, as in many other countries, most sociology researchers are university professors. Therefore, the system of research and education in universities must be reformed to promote the development of sociology. Until recently, Japan maintained the pre-war tradition of positioning sociology as a subdivision of philosophy departments within literature faculties. In recent years, sociology departments have emerged, and at the graduate level, sociology is increasingly separating from the humanities in the narrow sense to form independent graduate schools of sociology. This trend should be further promoted, and sociology should be given an appropriate position as a social science within all universities. While cooperation with the humanities remains important, it would be more beneficial to facilitate collaboration with economics, political science, and law.

Furthermore, sociology courses in national universities should become experimental courses, allowing for systematic survey research. This should extend to private universities as well, with hopes for more regular annual research funding than currently available. These studies are supported by Grants-in-Aid for Scientific Research (KAKENHI) from the Japan Society for the Promotion of Science (JSPS) and grants from various private organizations.

CURRENT STATE OF THE SOCIOLOGICAL COMMUNITY AND INTERNATIONAL EXCHANGE

Since 1965, Japanese sociology has developed both quantitatively and qualitatively. This development was driven by a dramatic increase in researchers compared to the pre-war period. When the new university system began in 1950, the number of professors specializing in sociology increased several times compared to pre-war levels. In these universities, sociology was taught as a social science during the first two years of general education. While not all universities had full-time sociology professors, and some courses were taught by professors from related fields or part-time lecturers, this increase in universities expanded the pool of sociology researchers.

The new graduate school system began in 1953, and around 1960, graduates from these programs began taking teaching positions in sociology. This led to a rapid increase in the number of young researchers over the next decade. From the late 1950s through the high-growth period of the 1960s, media theory, theories of Japanese society, and social consciousness theory gained attention. The expansion of higher education and the post-war baby boom combined to lead to university growth and the creation of new teaching positions.

Subsequently, in the 1970s, female researchers began feminist studies, pioneering today's gender theory perspective. The 1990s were marked by major domestic and international events such as the end of the Cold War, the collapse of the bubble economy, the Great Hanshin-Awaji Earthquake, and the Aum Shinrikyo incident. Intellectuals with backgrounds in sociology, which provided a comprehensive view of social pathology, became prominent, and it was sometimes called 'the era of sociology.' Furthermore, cultural studies examining popular culture brought fresh perspectives to Japanese pop culture research. Entering the 2000s, empirical research on inequality and disparities became a topic of interest. In recent years, both large-scale statistical surveys and qualitative research reproducing the narratives of ordinary people have attracted attention.

Currently, the Japan Sociological Society has approximately 3600 members. Their research fields have become increasingly diverse, with discussions on family, stratification, ethnicity, social pathology, education, culture, and theory taking place in over 70 sections. In addition to the Japan Sociological Society, regional sociological societies (Hokkaido, Tohoku, Kanto, Kansai, Western, etc.) also hold annual conferences.

Besides *Shakaigaku Hyoron*, other comprehensive sociological journals include *Soshioroji*, *Shakaigaku Kenkyu*, *Nenpoh Shakaigaku Ronshu*, *Sociologos*, and *Shakai to Chousa*. Specialized research organizations have formed in various fields, such as family research, rural society research, criminal sociology, and social psychology research. These groups collaborated with researchers in related fields and regularly presented research findings. Specialized academic societies continue to emerge and persist to this day, including the Society of Economic Sociology, The Japan Association for the Study on the History of Sociology, Japanese Association for Mathematical Sociology, and Japanese Association for Environmental Sociology (https://jss-sociology.org/9038-2/).

CONCLUSION: THE FUTURE DIRECTION OF JAPANESE SOCIOLOGY

Looking at the membership trends in the Japanese Sociological Society, there was steady growth until 2010. From this perspective alone, one might be optimistic about the future of Japanese sociology. However, there are several challenges that cannot be overlooked. Let us conclude by listing several key challenges facing Japanese sociology.

The first is the establishment of a fundamental systematic sociological theory. Post-war sociology was temporarily captivated by Parsonian sociology, likely due to the appeal of his social systems theory as an analytical framework ranging from basic units of action to whole-society level analysis. Its influence persists today. While there is substantial high-quality research on individual theorists like Parsons, Habermas, and Luhmann, reflecting a strong interest in general theory, there are no researchers attempting to construct theoretical systems that surpass these thinkers. We need bold new theoretical proposals from which higher-level sociological theories can emerge.

Second, while theoretical and historical studies remain relatively subdued, empirical research continues to accumulate daily. Surveys are conducted, and solutions are proposed for various social issues in Japan and worldwide. These naturally represent partial views of 'society.' These partial views should be coherently integrated to present a broader picture of Japanese and global society. Eitaro Suzuki started with Japanese village studies, expanded his scope to urban sociology and national sociology, and proposed a sociology encompassing all of Japan. Similarly, Yasuma Takata presented a sociology that conceived of class, nation, national community, and world society from the perspective of social bonds. These predecessors' comprehensive approaches to sociology can serve as valuable references.

Third, Japanese sociology must strive for internationalization. As mentioned earlier, some scholars publish research in foreign journals. However, given the quantity and quality of Japanese sociology, these international publications are far too few. While books in European languages by Japanese authors have begun to appear, they are overwhelmingly scarce considering the number of Japanese sociologists. The Japanese Sociological Society publishes two major academic journals in English: the *Japanese Sociological Review*, which contains Japanese articles with English abstracts and titles, and the *International Journal of Japanese Sociology*, published annually since 1992. For now, we must continue to assert the presence of Japanese sociology in these journals. The 2014 International Sociological Association conference in Yokohama attracted 6000 sociologists from around the world, with about 850 presentations from Japan. The Japan Sociological Society marked its 100th anniversary in 2024. Such international engagement must continue for the benefit of sociologists both in Japan and around the world (Yazawa, 2014).

REFERENCES

Kitagawa, R. (1965). Shakaigaku No Hoho [Methods of Sociology]. In *Gendai Shakaigaku Koza [Lectures on Contemporary Sociology]* (Vol. 1). Aoki Shoten. (In Japanese).

Tanaka, S. (1965). Kagakuteki Shakaisyugi and Kyosanshugi wo megutte [Concerning the Problems of Scientific Socialism and Communism]. In *Gendai Shakaigaku Koza [Lectures on Contemporary Sociology]* (Vol. 3). Aoki Shoten. (In Japanese).

Usui, J. (1975). Tsuiso [Reminiscences]. In *Kansai Shakaigakkai no Ayumi [History of the Kansai Sociological Society]*. Kansai Sociological Society. (In Japanese).

Yazawa, S. (2014). Five Meanings of 18th World Congress of Sociology: From Historical Perspective. *Japanese Sociological Review, 65*(3), 317–326.

Index[1]

[1] Note: Page numbers followed by 'n' refer to notes.

The manufacturer's authorised representative in the EU is Springer
Nature Customer Service Centre GmbH, Europaplatz 3, 69115 Heidelberg,
Germany. If you have any concerns regarding our products, please
contact ProductSafety@springernature.com

Printed and bound by CPI Group (UK) Ltd, Croydon, CR0 4YY

29/04/2026

02099450-0011